# Sea of Memories

STAN SMITH

 SPELLMOUNT LTD
Tunbridge Wells, Kent

**Stan Smith would like to thank Tony Clarke for all his help in the compilation of this book.**

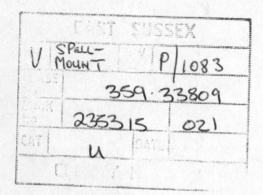

© Stan Smith 1985
First published UK in 1985 by
Spellmount Ltd
12 Dene Way, Speldhurst
Tunbridge Wells, Kent TN3 0NX
Designed by Sue Ryall

ISBN 0–946771–18–9 (UK)

Typeset by Wyvern Typesetting Limited, Bristol
Printed and bound by Anchor Brendon Ltd
Tiptree, Colchester, Essex.

# Contents

# Preface

The first half of the twentieth century contained some of the most dramatic events of world history – so far.

Through two world wars and countless smaller conflicts the great grey arms of the Royal Navy – the world's most formidable fighting fleet at the start of the century – embraced the globe.

No corner of the world was beyond the reach of those arms, no ocean free from the presence of great British ships.

But the Royal Navy was made up of men; men who were in the thick of the action; drawn together by firm bonds of comradeship; men whose pride in their ships was laced with a chirpy sense of humour; men who were not concerned with the politics of great world issues but with doing their job – whatever it might be and wherever it might take them – as professionally, and as cheerfully, as possible.

Men like STAN SMITH.

An East Anglian – just like that other great sailor before him, Lord Nelson (in fact, Nelson's parents were married in the Parish Church at Stan's home town of Beccles, in Suffolk) – Stan Smith ran away from home, lied about his age, and joined the Royal Navy.

From being 'button boy' at HMS *Ganges*, the East Coast shore training establishment, he went on to serve in the famous Q Ships – disguised merchantmen which were, in reality, warships – and to be badly wounded at Jutland, the last great clash between high seas fleets.

Survivor of the 'Black Hole of Baku', the infamous Bolshevik prison camp in Georgia, Stan came back from the dead to join an expedition into the remotest heart of the Amazon jungle in search of the lost explorer, Colonel Fawcett.

There is adventure in this story; there is colour and life too; vivid reconstructions, in Stan's own words, of what it was like to serve in His Majesty's ships when Britain really did rule the waves and memories of the seamier side in far flung ports.

Stan's words breathe life into the China Station and the South American ports visited during the 'Jam Commission' in days when sailors were away from home on commissions lasting two and a half years and more.

Famous ships – *Orion, Ramillies, Cumberland, Southampton* – sail through these pages. Old shipmates are recalled, along with their hair-raising exploits both in action and in fun.

Stan Smith – loyal sailor, patriot, incurable volunteer, adventurer, sometimes mischief maker, devoted husband and father – survived it all to reach those mature years of reflection.

And in the quietness of his bungalow, in his home town ten miles or so from the sea, Stan remembers those turbulent years which flowed together into his own personal Sea of Memories.

These pages are the result of his decision to share those memories with the world.

TONY CLARKE

# 1 · A Son of The Falcon

Right in the heart of East Anglia lies Beccles, the town which, to me, has always been home, however far I have travelled. It sort of fits me pretty much like a comfortable, warm, well 'run-in' jersey on a cold night at sea.

We've got a lot in common, this town and me. We're neither of us young any more; we've both seen hard times and been knocked around a bit, and we both try to wear our increasing 'maturity' with a smiling face.

Generations of East Anglians have been either men of the soft rolling fertile farmlands or seafarers. Whichever they are, they have been employed in a calling from which a living does not come easily.

Like the sturdy grey old church tower that stands up in the centre of my home town and dominates the countryside around, the character of the people of Beccles contains a sort of weather-beaten obstinacy, a tendency to dig your heels in and stand firm on the foundation of what you believe in, whatever anybody else may say.

At Beccles, the narrow streets and weathered old buildings provide a scene of more than passing interest to the holiday 'skippers' who now come up the River Waveney in their centrally heated Broads cruisers where once the little cargo coasters and wherries brought another kind of trade to the town.

A busy town, it is a place you have to come back to. We sit here beside our river, the border between Norfolk and Suffolk, surrounded by ever changing countryside, and close enough to the coast for an old salt to scent the sea in the air and hear, occasionally, the strident call of the gulls.

I am not a man of many words, but, laid up now in my home port, how can I resist the scent of the sea which brings so many memories of a life of adventure, of imprisonment and torture in far away places, of great ships and battles which now have a place only in the history books, of the grim humour and ready friendship of good men long gone?

But it isn't a story; it really happened and I thank God I survived, for many of my old shipmates never lived to tell the tale.

There's a saying round here – that we don't have much money but we see life. Right now, there's more fresh air than anything else in my britches pockets, but I have certainly seen life since that day when I ran away from home and joined the Royal Navy.

I've seen death too; violent, unnecessary suffering and death which is the only sure result of war. And I've seen courage, the sort of courage which, for the men of my Navy was just a matter of doing your job whenever and wherever it might take you.

But all this was part of my unknown future on 23 March 1899, when I first qualified as a resident of Beccles. I was born in a pub, which is as good a place as any to start life and to spend some of its happier moments later on!

The Falcon, an old coaching inn, has long since disappeared from the centre of the town, but in those days it was a place of some notoriety, and once or twice a week its basement cockpit was still the scene of regular cock fights.

My life of travel started when I was only two months old. My parents wanted a chance to build up their home, and since I must already have been proving a bit of a liability in this respect, I was duly removed to Great Yarmouth, about 12 miles away, to be brought up by my grandparents.

There, and I've got to admit it, I was spoilt. Not only did my grandmother and grand-dad make a great fuss of me, but I also enjoyed the attention of my nanny, Jenny Minns, whose main job seems to have been to take me out and about around the town.

As I grew older, I began to explore Yarmouth for myself – and it was very little like the busy hamburger, chips and bingo pleasure resort it is today.

The herring industry was at its height, the harbour filled with drifters, and horse trams ran through the centre of the town and along the promenade.

All the streets were cobbled and filled with horse-drawn carriages and carts.

My grandparents were very religious, and we went to church three times every Sunday. When I was old enough to go to school it was to the Priory School, run by the town's main parish church of St Nicholas, that I went.

We wore caps bearing three yellow rings and the Yarmouth coat of arms, and I recall, perhaps with some embarrassment, the rest of my first school uniform – velvet knee britches, shoes with a large silver buckle, a white lace shirt and collar and a small Eton jacket.

To complete this fashionable spectacle, my hair, which was in curls, flowed down to my waist, a memory which now gives cause for thought if I am ever tempted to pass comment on the unconventional 'rig' adopted by today's younger generation!

You could say that I represented the height of scholarly fashion, and when I was put into the choir of St Nicholas church, eventually to become chief solo boy, the limit of my infant ambition had been achieved.

After leaving the Priory School I was one of the first pupils at the Yarmouth Grammar School, which had just been completed. We had quite a lot of homework, which kept me fully occupied in the front parlour after school, and proved, in my case, an unexpected obstacle to academic progress.

Some kids are unlucky enough to have a teacher in the family. I had five of them, and they were all maiden aunts whose professional inclinations prevented them from helping me with my homework but certainly encouraged them to criticise it after I had finished.

After I left school they bought me an apprenticeship as an electrical engineer. Electricity had only just arrived at Yarmouth, the trams were all being converted from horse power and ours was one of the first houses to have 'the electric'.

But before I got lit up, electrically speaking, I was to return, temporarily, to the life of a publican. An Uncle and Aunt of mine kept the *Black Horse*, Earlham Road, Norwich, another of East Anglia's old pubs of character.

However, there was not much time for me to enjoy the experience. In those days, pub opening hours were from 6 o'clock in the morning to midnight – ideal for the drinkers but long days and damned hard work for the likes of me.

In any case, I was beginning to get other things on my mind. It was during my time in Norwich that the first World War broke out, and the first effect this had on me was to get me sent back to Yarmouth.

The whole population seemed to be caught up in war fever. All the young men were rushing to join up with the Forces for everybody said the war would only last six months at the most, and it seemed like a good thing to be part of it.

Swept along on this tide of feeling were two 15 year old youths filled with a determination to help the war effort in whatever way they could.

My old mate, Charlie White, and I had been 'partners in crime' at school together. We were, you might say, a well established and successful team when it came to doing the sort of things which were not necessarily viewed with favour by our families or teachers.

We did our best to join the Army, but we were 15 and enthusiasm wasn't enough. In fact, we got the distinct impression that they weren't *that* hard up for recruits!

But one evening, just as it was getting dark, a Zeppelin appeared over Yarmouth and dropped a number of bombs which did a bit of damage to the fish market and surrounding buildings.

This made us more than ever determined to join up and do our bit. We fished around for information and found out that we could join the Royal Navy at 15 years and three months.

Well, three months weren't going to make a lot of difference, so we went to war by tram, bound for the nearest Royal Navy recruiting office which had been set up in the Coastguard Station at Gorleston.

Faced by the irresistible enthusiasm of Charlie White and Stan Smith, the recruiting officer hadn't a chance. He agreed that we could join, provided we passed the necessary examinations and got our papers filled in and signed by our parents.

The first two qualifications were not too difficult to get over. We both survived a small educational test and were passed fit by the doctor.

Then came the problem. Charlie's parents were highly unlikely to sign his papers for him while I, with a doting grandmother and five maiden aunts to contend with, hadn't the ghost of a chance.

But Charlie and I had faced problems, and family disapproval, before and we hadn't been stumped for an answer yet. So, again, we rose to the occasion and, with the best of intentions, tried our hand at a bit of forgery. Charlie signed my papers and I signed his, on the principle, of course, that one good turn deserves another.

Back at the recruiting office our signatures were all unwittingly accepted as proof of parental approval, and we were told to report the following day with nothing more than the clothes we stood up in.

The next morning I left a note for my grandmother on the mantelpiece in my bedroom and slipped out to meet Charlie.

At Gorleston we were given railway warrants and a meal voucher. Then we were taken to Yarmouth station, put on a train and told to get off at Manningtree, in Essex.

From then on we were in the charge of a Petty Officer who took us by train to Harwich where we boarded a steam pinnance for the journey across to the Royal Navy training establishment at Shotley. We were in the Navy – and we had already been afloat.

# 2 · The Sail Makers

Thus, for better or worse, I had answered the call, whether from a sense of patriotism, shared with my contemporaries, or simply from a yearning for adventure I would not now hazard a guess.

At 15 I was truly on the threshold of life, and though I was soon to be plunged into the fearful reality of battle, to know real fear, hardship, injury and never-to-be-forgotten comradeship, I could only dream of what lay ahead.

But more pressing, on that first day at Shotley, was the need to eat, and what would the Royal Navy have to offer Charlie and me, its two newest and most raw recruits?

A meal of two boiled eggs and two thick slices of bread and butter was not the sort of thing I had been used to at home, but it filled an empty belly and I was glad of it.

Then, duly refuelled and ready for whatever the Navy had to offer, Charlie and I were shown the dining hall and the dormitory, and then allowed to wander around the barracks to get acquainted with the classrooms and other buildings.

The following morning we were called at 6.0 am, given a basin of cocoa and two biscuits and told we had fifteen minutes in which to wash, dress and fall in for P.T.

We joined the rest of the boys for P.T. on the football ground, and then had to run round the pitch for half an hour before being allowed to go in for breakfast.

After the meal we were examined by the doctor and the dentist, and later it was the turn of the barber to administer a close cropped hairstyle. There was no room for curly locks in the Navy of those days, for it was unanimously believed that ears should be well and truly seen.

So ended our first full day and the real business of training to be a sailor was about to begin with our introduction, next morning, to Petty Officer Slyfield.

There were twelve in our class and it didn't take any of us long to realise that Petty Officer Slyfield was a sailor of the old school, a tough old salt who believed that sailors were not born but hewn out by the vigorous application of discipline.

He would walk around carrying a six-inch vent bit – a thin steel rod about three foot long – which he would lay on to us with the utmost enthusiasm and the minimum of provocation.

Even before we started drilling he had given us his opinion, not only of ourselves but also of our mothers and fathers, whoever and whatever they might be. He even was inclined to doubt whether we had any at all.

Once we were at drill he exhibited an ability to swear which, in my experience, has never been equalled; a command of language which was, in itself, a part of my education which left a lasting impression.

But his job was to make sailors of us, and quickly, for there was a war on. And, for our part, we got on with the job. We learned gunnery, signalling, wireless and many other mysteries of life at sea. ´

Using a mock loader in the six-inch gun battery we had to heave projectiles weighing 100lb on to the loading tray, a feat of strength which taxed our young muscles to the utmost.

But we managed, after a fashion, and we got used to being called names – and we eventually passed all our subjects, an achievement which may well have been as much of a surprise to me as it was to Petty Officer Slyfield.

Having reached the dizzy heights of second class boy, I was able to exercise my new-found authority by marching the class from one classroom to another. But any delusions of grandeur were quickly to be demolished in the Shotley swimming pool.

We had to strip naked at one end of the baths and, seated on stools, received instruction on how to kick our arms and legs. Thus fortified with such basic theory, we had to parade at the six-foot end and jump in, one at a time.

It was at this point that I first began to understand the fear of the deep and to wonder whether the chief danger to my chances of survival came, not from the enemy, but from our side.

Survival, in fact, was the incentive to learn to swim. The instructor patrolled the edge of the baths armed with a long pole, and the swimmer's only reward for grabbing this was to be pushed under again.

You just had to grin and bear it – and kick and struggle to get to the other end. The fact that I'm still here proves that I made it, but there is little doubt that I was more drowned than alive.

After a few lessons came an even greater trial, a swimming test which we each had to endure wearing a canvas suit.

In the water these suits stiffened up tremendously and arms and legs also grew stiff and sore as we hapless water babies kicked our laborious way for two lengths of the baths. How I did it, I don't know, but the important thing was that I passed the test.

As my service wore on, I was going to realise, perhaps, the value of this rigorous training, for when a ship goes down and you've got to swim for it there is no time for the niceties of more leisurely instruction.

The next stage of our training came on board the old HMS *Ganges*, a sailing warship which, moored in the centre of the river, bore a name which was later to be inherited by the Shotley training establishment itself.

Her chief role, in those days, was to teach us seamanship. We had to learn how to control and use oars in the various boats, including gigs, skiffs, whalers and cutters.

We did no P.T. in the mornings, but we had to go over the masthead instead – and that was a jolly sight worse. The ratlines were made of half-inch thick tarred rope, and we had to go over bare footed.

They cut our feet to pieces and we were glad to come down the other side on our knees.

We also had to go out on the fotting rigging which ran out from the shrouds to the edge of the crow's nest. Out on this rigging we were at an angle of 45 degrees so it was important not to lose grip with our feet. This would have left us hanging in mid-air.

The only way to avoid the fotting rigging was to escape through the lubber's hole in the centre near the mast, but neither the discipline nor our own fear of failure allowed us to use this bolt hole.

I became quite expert at climbing the rigging. With one or two others, I used to climb the mast in my spare time and get in the crow's nest for a smoke.

This was one of my first experiences of 'bending' the Royal Navy rules – and getting away with it – for we weren't officially allowed to smoke until we were 18.

But the practice of climbing the mast – however illegally gained – stood me in good stead. When we had ceremonial occasions I was chosen as 'button boy', which meant that I had to climb the mast and stand on the cap at the very top.

It is possible to get used to heights and I got so confident that there was no fear at all in standing on a platform which was, I suppose, about one and a half foot square.

It looks so small from the ground far below, but one and a half foot is quite a big area to stand on, even if the platform seems to be surrounded by nothing but fresh air, and the people way down there look very small indeed.

We were each issued with two hammocks, a set of clews and a lashing. Then we were taught how to point and put an eye in the lashing and how to sling the hammocks using a simple half-hitch which tightened up with the increasing weight put on it.

There was, as you may guess, a good deal of fun when we got into our hammocks for the first time. Some went straight over the top while others were swallowed up like Egyptian mummies. But we eventually got the hang of it.

To be fair, we were each also issued with a bed, two covers and two blankets.

Then, as we gradually began to feel, and perhaps even to look, more like sailors, we were kitted out for sea.

They gave us four of everything – underclothing, white suits, navy suits, collars and the like. Our equipment included a 'housewife', a pad containing needles, cotton, and all the necessities for patching up our clothes. This pad could be rolled up and tied with two tapes.

Naturally our gear had to be marked and I spent some time attaching a piece of wood with my name cut into it to my gear. Navy coloured items had to be marked with white paint, and white things with black paint and our boots and shoes acquired metal identification discs.

We were then shown how to lay these things out for kit inspection, Royal Navy style.

Basic instruction on how to wash our clothes and keep ourselves fit and clean was not forgotten and we were also put into messes where we had to make our own tea and peel our own spuds, just as we would have to do on board our first ship.

Hammocks, though very nice to sleep in, posed a special problem in the mornings. Called at 6.0 am, we had to jump out smartly and lash our hammocks with seven complete half-hitches, all exactly the right distance apart, before stowing them away.

Only then could we get away for our basins of cocoa and couple of biscuits, get washed, and be ready, 20 minutes later, for what the day might bring.

When the Petty Officer came round in the morning with his 'Wakey, wakey' call, it was a scramble that could only be seen to be believed.

Such was my life on board the old HMS *Ganges*, a life so different from the cosy existence I had known before, but so very much a preparation for a new life of discovery to come.

Back in Great Yarmouth, my 'battalion' of aunts had never really got over the shock of my sudden departure into the arms of the Royal Navy. Nor had they given up the battle to make me see the error of my ways.

In fact, Aunts Ethel and Mary, believing, no doubt, that no battle can be won without a formidable offensive, even advanced on Shotley itself, going straight to the Commanding Officer in an attempt to buy me out.

When the C.O. sent for me I was faced with a decision, and an opportunity, had I wanted it, to go home. But, maybe my training had done its job too well, stiffening my resolve to the point where nobody was ever going to call me a quitter.

I looked at my aunts and I looked at the Navy – and I stayed put.

I was soon convinced that the decision had been right, for the great thrill of my young life came with the news of my first draft, to the famous HMS *Orion*, flagship of the 2nd Battle Squadron.

*Orion* – that was a name to conjure with. Not surprisingly. I was buoyed up by excitement as I packed my bags, lashed my hammocks and got my gear loaded on to the pinnace which was to take me ashore.

The journey by train from Harwich to London and then on to Thurso, the topmost port in Scotland, seemed interminable for it was taking me to a great ship in waters which have a special place in the history of the British Isles – Scapa Flow.

# 3 · The Mighty *Orion*

Only an old sailor can share the thrill of that boat journey which gave me my first sight of Scapa Flow, and there, in the heart of a mass of great grey ships, HMS *Orion*.

My eyes swallowed up every detail of her heavily armoured bulk and her ten 13.5 inch guns. I knew enough about her to understand that she could reach a speed of 21 knots, and that the armour cladding on her sides was about 11 inches thick.

But I was not so much bothered about her vital statistics as eager to learn what sort of a life she was to offer me at sea.

Once on board, the new arrivals were told off for their action stations, cruising stations, and directed to the part of the ship to which they were to belong.

I was a foretopman, and my action station was in 'B' turret operating a clockwork arrangement which gave the rate of change, increase or decrease, of an enemy ship.

At sea we were closed up pretty often at action stations. In fact, I ate my first Christmas dinner at sea – corned beef and biscuits – closed up in 'B' turret.

On return to harbour, the first job was to coal ship. This involved all the ship's company, nobody was excused.

When the collier came alongside the fo'castleman would man its first hold, the foretopman the second, the maintopman the third and the quarterdeck man the last hold.

They would fill up bags held by the boys who also had to pass strops through the handles of the bags so that about twenty at a time could be lifted by the hoist and dumped down on the ship. Men with trolleys and barrows would then run them away to the nearest shute.

If the ship had been at sea for some time she would probably need between four and five thousand tons of coal.

The boys had the worst job of all. Each one held a bag with five or six men shovelling coal into it as fast as they could. Dust got into your

17

mouth, in your eyes, up your nose and into every other known and unknown place.

After coaling, but before you were allowed to go for a bath, the nets had to be got out. These were heavy steel mesh nets that hung down from the waterline to about the depth of the ship.

They were held in position by a series of booms about 14ft long, and these booms were, in turn, held in place by topping lifts and shrouds so that they stood out horizontal from the ship.

The idea of this defensive arrangement was that, if an enemy submarine crept into Scapa and fired a torpedo at you, it would hit the netting and explode without damaging the hull of the ship.

But ideas are all very well and have only a limited life in wartime. The Germans, as inventive as the British when it came to solving defensive problems, fitted a cutting device to their torpedoes so, after a while, the nets were useless and were scrapped.

In any case, after coaling ship, we could well do without the extra job of getting out the nets for we still had to clean the ship before we could get round to the job of cleaning ourselves. The Navy had its priorities right; ship first, self second – and a very poor second at that!

Every spot of coal dust had to be cleared away and washed out of every corner of the ship, and all the paintwork had to be washed down before the ship's company, to its utmost relief, was allowed an hour in which to bath and wash its coaling gear.

So far as the ship's sixty boys were concerned, even this operation was not exactly carried out in five-star comfort. The word bathroom hardly described accurately the cubby hole in which we carried out our ablutions.

There were no baths, just buckets and so great was the pressure on space that bath time resembled a huge rugby scrum with a mass of heaving, shoving, sweating bodies scrambling for the buckets.

If you were lucky enough to get near enough, the most you could hope for was to get one foot in the bucket and wash half of yourself before pushing and shoving to get the other foot in and finish the job.

But worse was to come. I was, at the time, engaged in seamanship training which involved instruction in such relatively civilised skills as wire splicing, rope splicing and rigging derricks and sheer legs. But this was to be followed by one month of stoke hole training.

Considering our primitive bathroom arrangements, we boys probably could be excused for wondering why we happened to get all the dirty jobs in the stoke hole! We were to be found cleaning out the bilges and going inside the boilers to scrape the scum off – activities from which we emerged even grimier than ever.

At sea our main job was to keep the stokers fully supplied with coal. At the mouth of each shute we filled mobile skips which we then wheeled across to the stokers so that they could shovel the coal into the furnaces.

At the best of times this was a hot and grimy job which brought us into contact with a tough breed of men who sweated bare-backed in the bowels of the ship and rarely went topsides to smell the sea. Their domain was a kind of hell made even worse when the crash of gunfire and exploding shells meant the ship was in action. There was no comfort to know that you were perpetually below the waterline.

When the sea was lumpy our job became a wrestling match with skips which seemed to have a will of their own, running all over the place, and always, it seemed, in the wrong direction. As we strained and fought to control them, we had one thought in our minds; our stoke hole training was drawing to a close.

For me, it was followed by three months of destroyer training, and I was transferred to HMS *Spitfire*, one of the squadron's smaller destroyers.

I soon found that life on board a destroyer was quite different from that in a battleship. The discipline was still there, but it was less formal and, in this smaller community, every member of the ship's company felt very much a part of the 'family'. Life had its humour and the leg-pulling was plentiful.

In fact, it was on board the *Spitfire* that I was to learn what the comradeship of the sea really meant and, in due course, to receive my first scars of battle in that famous but inconclusive Battle of Jutland.

# 4 · The Battle of Jutland

While at sea one day on patrol we found five or six bodies floating in the ocean. We picked them up, took off their identification discs, so that relatives could be informed, and were then told off in pairs to sew the bodies up in canvas and place a weight at their feet for burial at sea after a short service.

I was told off with an able seaman to do the job on a Lascar. As we turned this poor chap over on his back on the destroyer's hot deck the air came out of him in a loud grunt. By gosh, I was scared.

I was away and as fast and as far forward as possible and it was about an hour before I got over the shock. I was young and inexperienced and had never seen a dead body before so, although I was later to see many more dreadful sights, this is an experience I shall never forget.

On 31 May 1916 we were at sea escorting the Fifth Battle Squadron when the signal was passed round that the German High Seas Fleet had come out at last. Though we did not know it at the time, this was to be the Battle of Jutland.

The squadron engaged battleships of the *Kaiser* Class and the shells were soon screaming overhead. Now and again, a shell would fall some 50 or 60 yards from us, and we were living dangerously for destroyers were only built of quarter-inch thick plate and it did not take much to demolish one.

We continued escorting during the afternoon and there was intermittent firing till nightfall when we were ordered to make a destroyer attack on the High Seas Fleet.

A destroyer attack is often carried out at night and you steam straight for the enemy lines. When you are within a few thousand yards you turn, fire your torpedoes, make a smokescreen and get to hell out of it.

We steamed straight for the German lines and it seemed almost as if we were going to touch them before the order was given to fire torpedoes and we turned and fired.

Up to that point we had not been spotted but the act of firing pinpointed us for the Germans. In those days torpedoes were not fired by compressed air but by a cordite charge which gave off a tremendous flash.

We were spotted on the turn, and before our smokescreen could cover us, all hell broke loose.

We were hit several times. I was on the after gun, which was on a 'bandstand' raised some three feet from the deck.

It was a four-inch gun and as site-setter I was tucked away right inside the shield. It was a devil of a job to get out.

The shell that did the damage to us on the gun hit the searchlight tower just 'forrard' of the bandstand and when it exploded it threw the whole gun completely over on its side; shield, mounting, the lot.

I was slung over with it and it was quite some time before I managed to get clear. When I eventually got out I found that all the rest of the gun's crew had been killed; some blown almost to pieces.

It was then that I felt conscious of a pain in my leg. Taking my shoe off, I found it was full of blood – and I fainted.

When I came to, I was on the mess deck. In a destroyer we had no sick bay accommodation for anybody who was ill or wounded. There was only our hammocks.

I was on my hammock which had been spread out along the lockers which contained our clothes and also formed seats for us to sit at the table.

Our doctor was the coxswain. He had been given some first aid training and that was all.

He did what he could for all the wounded and we were also in communication with the big ships for any special job that needed doing for the worst wounded.

I learned afterwards that the damage to our ship was quite considerable. Half the fo'c'stle had been blown in and there was a large hole on the starboard side over which a collision mat had to be fitted.

One set of torpedo tubes had been blown clean out of the ship and one of the propeller shafts had been bent and broken so that we could only use one screw.

Our ship was ordered to return to base. But it was so badly damaged that, at one point, as we limped our way back to Glasgow, water was coming in where the collision net had been fitted, so fast that we had to go stern first for several miles until the mat had been re-arranged.

Snug in my hammock, and waiting to go to hospital, I was spared all this excitement.

On arrival at Glasgow the ship went straight into dock and the wounded went straight to the General Hospital, where I was put in an annexe.

My leg was a sorry mess. Part of the shin had been blown away and the doctors fitted a silver plate and grafted the flesh and skin over the top.

Considering all things, I was quite comfortable in hospital. The doctors and nurses did a marvellous job; especially the nurses.

We had two favourites. One we called Battling Joe Beckett because she was always squaring you up, tucking in your coverlet and always making you look neat and tidy, regardless of how ill you might be feeling.

The other, we called the Angel of Mons. She was lovely. She did everything possible to make us comfortable.

She didn't worry about our coverlets, or anything like that, but would give you a cigarette or sweet or just pass the time of day and make you feel better just by doing so.

In all, I was in hospital just over two months, and when I left, I was returned to Chatham Barracks and given seven days leave.

This took me back to Norwich to visit my Aunt and Uncle at the BLACK HORSE public house – but even there I couldn't keep clear of the action.

Walking along College Road, in Norwich, one day, I saw a man with a horse and cart trying to get up the hill. He was beating the poor animal unmercifully and it was struggling, often going down on its knees.

I saw red, grabbed the whip from the chap and started on him with it, until a policeman appeared, as if from nowhere.

We all joined forces, the three of us pushing at the back and the horse pulling, to heave the load to the top of the hill.

The policeman took our names and we thought that was the end of the incident.

But not on your life! On the last day of my leave I had to go back to Norwich to appear before the magistrates.

I was highly commended for stopping the brutality to the horse, but fined ten bob for taking the law into my own hands.

However, on my return to barracks, there was better news on the financial front. I found I had been made Ordinary Seaman some two months previously and had a little back pay to come.

# 5 · The 'Q' Ships

It was at this time that the famous, and sometimes ill-fated, Q-ships came into my life when a notice went up asking for volunteers.

Q-ships were the Royal Navy's first answer to the menace of the submarine. They were dilapidated old merchant ships taken from the scrap heap and fitted up with concealed guns.

They were so old and decrepit that a submarine, it was thought, would not waste a torpedo on them, but would rely on gunfire to intimidate their crews into abandoning ship.

The theory was that when they had done this, the submarine would gradually circle the ship and eventually come alongside to loot the vessel for provisions.

I was chosen, and after passing a medical, we volunteers were kitted out with civilian clothing. I say 'kitted out', but we had to pass the things round to get a decent fit.

We were sent by train to West Hartlepool to join our ship, Q-12, which was quickly to prove that the Q-ship strategy didn't work out as planned.

She was a rough old vessel, eaten up with rust. But she had two 4-inch guns concealed under the bridge behind flaps which dropped down when the guns were needed.

On number three hatch a coil of manila rope would fall back at the pull of a lever to reveal a 12-pounder gun.

The control tower was located in a hawser reel on the fo'c'stle.

The ship was also fitted with bell pushes around the upper deck. The idea was that if you saw a periscope you would put your foot on a bell push and send everybody, unseen, to action stations. Then you would light a fag and stroll away casually to your own.

Q-12's mess decks were in a filthy condition so we turned to and scrubbed out, gathered up all the fish and chip papers, lunch bags, pieces of bread and butter and other litter, and made the mess decks fairly shipshape.

But all this activity didn't half get us wrong. It caused a dockyard strike.

It seemed that women were employed to clean the ships behind the dockyard people and we had done them out of a job.

But after some heated negotiations our Commanding Officer managed to square things up and they got back to work.

When she was completed in the dockyard, Q-12 had to go out to sea to swing compasses. The accuracy of these instruments was always affected by riveting or any changes in the ship's metal-work.

With one or two dockyard people still on board, we went out about twelve miles and were getting on quite well with swinging the compasses when – whoof! – a torpedo hit us amidships. I don't suppose she took more than two or three minutes to sink.

Floundering in the water, we were quickly picked up by boats from the shore and by a tug which had been escorting. But that was the end of the Q-12 without a shot fired in anger and with no opportunity to test the Navy's Q-ship strategy.

So, back to barracks we went, but it wasn't long before I got another Q-ship, again from West Hartlepool.

She was fitted out almost the same as the Q-12, except that instead of a 12-pounder being under the hawser reel it was in an upturned boat which was cut away in sections which fell away at the pull of a lever.

While in West Hartlepool, waiting for the ship to be completed, we would go ashore, although there was not much pleasure in it.

The girls, seeing you in 'civilians' and knowing you were of military age, would stick white feathers in your coats. In the public houses we invariably clued up in an argument about why we weren't in the Forces.

In fact, three of us went to a cinema one night and during the show the place was raided by civilian and military police, looking for men of military age.

We were taken to the police station and, since we were sworn to secrecy, our Commanding Officer had to come and bail us out.

When the ship was completed we finished with the dockyard and went to sea. Having swung compasses and carried out gun trials – this time uneventfully – we were on our own.

The unwieldy old vessel would plough up and down the length of England in the trade routes. Her screw and rudder were only one-third in the water, and, although she had ballast, she would spin and yaw all over the place in a strong wind and a decent sea.

Food was not too good, either. We only carried fresh provisions for five days and after that we would be on corned beef and biscuits.

We would dish up the corned beef in many and varied ways which would make today's food experts wince.

The biscuits were very hard and we would soak them overnight then strain them off and mix in a tin of suet, a few currants and a little sugar and bake the mixture, it was quite palatable then.

The routine had us doing about ten to twelve days at sea at a stretch before going in to coal and water. Coaling was quite easy because we would go under the chute.

But, wherever the story of Q-ships is told, the events of our second patrol should be recalled – for here was the Q-ship strategy at work with the enemy running true to form.

One of the chaps saw a periscope, put his foot on the alarm and sent us all to action stations.

The submarine cruised round the ship – which was quite easy since we were only doing about four knots – and had a good look at us.

The duty of one of the seamen, dressed as a woman, was to go up and hang out some washing on the fo'c'stle line. Having done this, he would go down and get to his action station.

The submarine surfaced about a mile away and opened fire. Now another of our little ploys came into play.

We had containers scattered around the ship which were electrically operated from the control tower. These could be activated to cause a miniature explosion, showering fire, sparks and smoke all over the show.

The idea of this was that if the submarine sent a shell over the ship she could be confused into thinking she had scored a hit. Being low in the water, she wouldn't be able to spot an 'over' if it was in line with the ship.

Her first couple of shells fell short. Then she got an 'over' which we immediately gave her as a 'hit'.

She carried on firing for some ten to fifteen minutes and did manage to knock the mast down and the derricks over the forward hold, but they didn't put the gun, hidden in the boat, out of action.

Next, we sent away the 'panic boats' and stopped the ship.

The panic boats' crew consisted of all men – stokers and so on – who were not manning the guns or the control.

They would dash up on deck, lower the boat haphazardly and with every sign of panic, and then jump in and pull away as fast as they could.

The submarine stopped firing and began to circle the ship, coming closer each time.

When she was about a hundred yards off the port beam and we could get two guns to bear on her – the 4-inch and the 12-pounder – we opened fire.

After the third or fourth salvo we sunk her and the panic boats' crews went over to her. There were only two survivors.

When we returned to port the Navy confirmed our claim. But, unfortunately, this was a short-lived success and our reign on board did not last long.

We were continually having engine trouble and, at times, could barely keep steerage way on. In any case, one day as we came into harbour to coal and water, against wind and tide, we hit the jetty and tore a large gash in the port side.

We hoped this would give us a few days leave but it was not to be. Instead, they paid her off and we were returned to Chatham Barracks.

My next ship was HMS *Montbretia* – totally different from the other two Q-ships.

She was a 17-knot sloop which had been converted to look like a merchantman. She had two 4.7-inch guns concealed under the bridge and a 12-pounder in an upturned boat, but she was fitted with all the latest controls.

She also had a listening device, the only snag being that you had to stop the ship to listen.

She was fitted with two depth-charge throwers, one on each side of the quarter-deck. Each was like a mortar and had a cradle into which the depth-charges were lashed.

I should imagine the depth-charges weighed just over a hundredweight. They were about the size of a large oil drum.

They could be set to explode at depths of 50ft to 250ft, but the snag was that these were a new invention and, like all new ideas, they didn't always operate as they should.

In fact, they would often explode on hitting the water, showering the ship with lumps of cradle and causing quite a bit of damage.

On one occasion an artificer was dodging round the funnel when he saw one of them explode. A piece of cradle hit him in the behind, making quite a nasty wound which put him in hospital.

We didn't have a lot of success with submarines although we claimed to have sunk one by depth-charges. Oil and debris came to the surface but the Navy would not confirm our claim.

It was pointed out that submarines could tell that we were not what we seemed because the beat of our screw was much faster than that of a merchant ship.

So we were put on convoy duty where we could fly the White Ensign, get back into uniform and show all the guns.

# 6 · Northern Patrol

The next memorable phase of my life at sea was Northern Patrol – but it was memorable for a variety of none-too-pleasant reasons.

Working from the Shetland Isles we were based at Lerwick, a truly one-horse town at that time, where the monotony was relieved only by the monthly visit of the beer boat.

A crowd of us would buy a small barrel and take it up into the hills for a drink.

Patrols, lasting from ten to twelve days, were pretty arduous. We not only had to contend with a lack of fresh provisions half the time, but also ice – tons of it.

Huge icicles hung from the rigging and upper works and we had to chop them off in the mornings to avoid carrying too much top weight. She carried quite a lot as it was and could roll like the very devil.

Look-outs were posted round the clock for we were in the 'Land of the Midnight Sun' and there was always enough daylight for a look-out to spot anything unusual.

One night the masthead look-out reported a submarine on the port bow. We were all sent to action stations and the ship turned full speed ahead to ram.

We duly rammed the 'vessel' just as the 'bow' was lifting from a large swell – and immediately wished we hadn't.

This was no sub, but a large whale that had been left by the whaling fleet after inflation, and heaven knows how long it had been floating around for it was white with seagull droppings.

Our supposed submarine, on being rammed, inevitably retaliated by showering the ship as far aft as the funnel – and, oh boy! what a stink!

The smell was atrocious. We couldn't get rid of it. It went down through the ventilators into the messdecks and I came the nearest I have ever been to getting sea-sick.

A month after this I was made an able-seaman and recommended to go to barracks to pass for seaman gunner.

Back at Chatham I joined the gunnery school for intensive training with all types of guns from 12-pounders to 15-inch. The first thing we were taught was that walking was not allowed in the precincts of the gunnery school.

Everything had to be done at the double and the first four weeks consisted of drill and very little else. We seemed to spend most of our time on the parade ground with our rifles and bayonets, doing all kinds of drill, both ceremonial and otherwise.

After this, we graduated into the heavy guns section where we learned about hydraulics, which was the method by which the guns were loaded.

We were taught how to load the guns, how to fuse the shells, what the shells were made of, and many other facts that a seaman gunner would need to know.

We were also initiated into the mysteries of the night shooting battery which simulated a ship at sea and in action in the dark. A small air rifle fixed to the big gun scored hits on miniature targets and indicated what damage would have been done by a shell.

In this way, any mistakes we made could be pin-pointed.

Next we spent a week in the ammunition section, learning all there was to know about the bullets and shells we actually fired, and the explosives which set them off.

The following week we went on board a tender and fired ten rounds of six-pounder and ten rounds of 12-pounder at a moving target towed by a trawler.

Next we went down to Sheerness for a week for rifle and revolver shooting on the range and you could earn yourself a little prize money if you got top score on the targets.

I didn't do so well with the rifle as I did when shooting the revolver for which I won myself the princely sum of 7s.6d; just 37½p in today's currency.

Passing top of the class for seaman gunner – though I shouldn't boast about it – I went back to the gunnery school for three weeks training to become a range finder operator, third class. This gave me an extra threepence a day.

It was only a matter of days after this that the Armistice was signed but I had no chance to celebrate for I was placed on immediate draft to HMS *Emperor of India*.

She was a battleship of the *Iron Duke* class. She had ten 13.5-inch guns, twelve 6-inch guns, four 4-inch anti-aircraft guns and numerous smaller weapons. She was also equipped with submerged torpedo tubes.

It was an emergency draft and almost as soon as the ship's company got on board we set sail for a secret and mysterious destination – .

# 7 · Debris of War

Up to now my time in the Royal Navy had all been spent in British Waters. The year was 1918, the war was over or so I thought, and a fairly uncomplicated life seemed to stretch ahead.

But life, especially in the Royal Navy, is always full of surprises. Sailing into the unknown in a ship with secret orders, Able Seaman Stan Smith was about to find out that, Armistice or no, the world was still full of people at war with each other.

Brief stops at Gibraltar and Malta, for oiling, neither provided us with any leave nor gave us a clue to our ultimate destination.

On we sailed through the Dardanelles to the entrance to the Bosphorus where, off Constantinople (now Istanbul), we dropped anchor.

The reason for our overseas dash then became clear for the Turks appeared to be in the process of massacring all the Germans and Armenians they could find.

I had no idea why they picked on the Armenians but the fact is that murderous parties roamed the streets by night, stringing people up by their feet on lamp-posts, slitting them up the middle and putting their testicles in their mouths.

I was eighteen at the time and it was a sight that I can never forget, however hard I try.

In this scene of horror and violence, we British sailors faced the none-too-easy job of finding and rounding up all the Germans that were left. Not surprisingly, they had scattered and were hiding in many remote corners of the city and, even when we found them we could not be sure that they would treat us with anything more than suspicion. After all, we had only recently fought against their country in the war to end all wars.

As we rounded them up we took them to a merchant ship which had been commandeered and anchored, for their own safety, in the middle of the Bosphorus.

Hunger, thirst and disease were as much enemies to the population

31

on shore as were the night-time murderers, for there was very little food and even less water.

On board the *Emperor of India* our bakers worked day and night and our engineers were kept busy round the clock distilling water.

As the supplies arrived on shore the starving people rushed and fought over them. Large armed parties of our ship's company struggled to keep some sort of order and to show the people that the only way to get anything was to queue for it.

Gradually, with the aid of our rifle butts and the occasional bayonet prod, we persuaded the queues to form and the food was distributed as fairly as we could manage.

Perhaps, partly as a result of this emergency service, things began to quieten down in Constantinople itself, and we were allowed on shore to visit places of interest, including the magnificent Mosque of St Sophia.

A certain amount of fraternisation developed between the British sailors and the local people, but not all of it was necessarily designed to win friends and influence people.

Some of the less scrupulous members of our ship's company, in fact, cottoned on to a particularly profitable exercise which was based largely on the fact that many of the people on shore had never seen a £1 note.

The labels on our tins of Ideal Milk were rather elaborate with the lettering intertwined in a gold coloured scroll. The lads promptly found a new use for these artistic labels, cutting them to the size of a £1 note and changing them at the local money market.

At first it seemed that our illicit currency was more popular than the genuine article and our financial wizards prospered for a time. But the ruse was soon exposed when the money men on shore found that our notes were not as 'ideal' as they seemed.

Perhaps we had outstayed our welcome. In any event, we were soon on our way into the Black Sea to lend support to Anton Ivanovich Denikin and the Tzarist Russians who were fighting the Bolsheviks.

In turn, we laid off Odessa, Yalta and Sebastopol, bombarding in support of the forces on shore.

At Sebastopol I had a chance to go ashore and visit the famous Round Tower. All around the interior was a massive painting of 'The Charge of the Light Brigade' from the Crimean War. It was a magnificent, almost indescribable, sight and I can only sit here at home now and remember – and hope that it is still there and feel proud my uncle Briggs was a survivor of the same.

It was also at Sebastopol that a Russian general came on board and, for reasons best known to himself, gave me a medal, a handshake and a kiss. Oh, the embarrassment of it! There was nothing in my Naval training to tell me how to cope with such affectionate advances from a high-ranking Russian Officer. However, discipline held firm and I was the proud possessor of the 5th Order of St George.

A total of five medals was issued to the ship by Denikin's forces and they were carefully – and thinly – distributed one to each department of a ship containing more than one thousand men. I received mine for being range-finder operator in the gun control.

I have to admit that this medal – or, rather, my disrespectful treatment of it – caused me a lot of trouble.

From our mess the cooks would send potatoes up to the galley in nets marked with a wooden tally. One day, when I was cook of the mess, I couldn't find a piece of wood anywhere, so I promptly put my medal on the spud net.

Up to the galley went the spuds and the medal. The chief cook spotted it, reported me, and I had seven days' leave stopped – due reward, perhaps, for the value I had placed on my Russian 'gong'.

What happened to the medal after that, I just don't know. Maybe it went overboard. Perhaps I tucked it away in my kit, which, in any case, was all lost later when I was a prisoner-of-war, but that, for the moment, is another story.

Anyway, we were soon leaving Sebastopol astern as we sailed back through the Bosphorus to the Dardanelles on a mission to help the Army to clear Gallipoli.

This took us right into another big mess on shore. Ammunition and bodies – skeletons mostly – lay everywhere and we were employed on the gruesome task of collecting up bones and skulls, often one skull to two shovelfuls of bones, and carting them in boxes to the top of a hill where the Army had cleared a space for a cemetery. There was many a poor soldier there whose grave was unknown and unmarked.

We also had to dispose of ammunition, exploding it or dumping it at sea to clear the island.

Faced with the same job on the ANZAC beaches where the Australians had lost a lot of men, we spent, in all, about ten days helping to clear up the fearsome 'litter' of war.

It is a task which I wouldn't wish on anyone; except, perhaps, the politicians whose decisions usually cause it all in the first place. This is the side of war which makes many an old sailor or soldier wince when brave words are spoken about honour and freedom; the grim face of glory.

It was with profound relief that we left Gallipoli for Malta where the ship was due for refit and we could look forward to a few days' leave.

A quiet interlude seemed in prospect but even here events immediately plunged yours truly straight into trouble again. We were hoisting out one of the boats when the block gave way and a piece of the cheek crashed down on to my dud leg.

Before you could say Jack Tar I was on my way to Bigi Hospital. It was no simple job for the doctors and nurses because they couldn't get the particles of flesh to close in over the plate which was my personal souvenir of Jutland.

Eventually, they would put tourniquets on my leg, initially for five minutes at a time and gradually working up to about twenty minutes. The pain would thump away in my head until I nearly went mad with it, but it did the trick and the flesh gradually crept up over the silver plate.

They would spray a kind of hot tallow on to my leg so that the particles of flesh would stay in place after the tourniquets were taken off. Then they took a piece of skin from my behind and grafted it over the wound to finish off what I must admit was a pretty good repair job.

After convalescence, I was sent to Europa Point Barracks to await the arrival of my ship but events were to take another unexpected turn and, for me, the *Emperor of India* was never to arrive.

As usual, it was all my own fault, of course. I had been laid up in hospital too long and I suppose I wanted to be back where the action was.

My opportunity came when a notice went up asking for volunteers for an expedition to Enzeli on the Caspian Sea.

Ignoring the old Service advice – never volunteer – I put my name forward because the expedition sounded rather interesting.

I was one of the few chosen and a new chapter of action, danger and imprisonment opened up for me; proving, perhaps, that Stan Smith is the sort of bloke who goes around followed by trouble. Only my survival indicated that somebody 'up there' must like me!

# 8 · Bandits and Bolsheviks

Like most sailors or soldiers, I was not greatly concerned with the politics of war. We left those to the politicians.

I was there to do a job and, in the situation in which I found myself, it was not entirely relevant who was fighting whom. So I can only relate my story as I remember it happening and leave the history of wars and the reasons for them to others better qualified to explain the strategy behind the great issues of the day.

We were a motley crowd of twenty-nine volunteers. There were one or two from each branch of the Services, and after being pronounced fit by the 'medic', we were kitted out in khaki.

Well, a laugh now and again is as good a tonic as any I can think of, and I had plenty of laughs during my life at sea. I have only to remember the fun we had wrestling to get into our puttees – a form of dress entirely new to me at the time – to get a good few chuckles as I sit at home now and remember.

We also acquired pith helmets with an attachment known to us as a buggery – an apt title if ever there was one. It was, in fact, a length of muslin attached to the helmet and designed to encircle it several times, crossing both at the front and the back. It was a devil of a job to get rigged up in it.

We soon formed a great respect for our Commanding Officer, Commander Bruce Fraser, and I have retained that sense of respect ever since for I regard myself privileged to have served with him. He was later to become Admiral Sir Bruce Fraser and he commanded the Fleet at the time of the sinking of the battleship *Scharnhorst* during the Second World War.

A destroyer took us back up through the Dardanelles and the Bosphorus to the Black Sea port of Batumi. That was as far as the ship could take us and our next conveyance was a train.

Consisting of an engine and three wagons with sliding doors each side, not unlike the covered goods trucks seen in England, this was not exactly an Inter-City express and I doubt if British Rail have often encountered the sort of hazards which came our way.

We loaded up all the equipment we would need for repairing such things as guns and engines and started the long ride to the Caspian Sea. We were not to reach our destination that time for yours truly was about to meet up with bandits for the first time in his young life.

Two days out from Batumi we were in the foothills of the Caucasian Mountains when the train ground to a halt. There was a blockage on the line and we were on the receiving end of a very efficient ambush.

Coming under fire from bandits hidden in the hills we flung open the wagon doors, built barricades with our kitbags and hammocks, and returned the rifle fire.

The exchanges intensified until the fight was hotting up on both sides of the track. The engine driver refused to go on even if the blockage was cleared so, there we were – stuck.

There was no chance of going forward and it was certainly too hot to stay where we were so we had no alternative but to reverse – I won't use the word retreat. Anyway, two days later we were back in Batumi, a little older and a lot wiser.

Our stores were loaded on board another ship and we were taken back through the Black Sea and the Bosphorus to Izmir on the Turkish coast, in the Sea of Marmara.

There we were to become rail 'commuters' again, bound for Baghdad. But that was the end of the line and from Baghdad there was no choice but to start a long, long walk.

Our stores and equipment were loaded on to camels and we began to footslog our way across Persia, a prospect which held little appeal for a chap with a silver plate in his leg.

As if this wasn't bad enough we were now to meet up with camp thieves – well, not exactly meet up with them for they visited us by night and vanished into the wide open spaces by day.

It was incredible. We could see quite ten to fifteen miles across open country during the day, but there was never a soul in sight. At night our unknown and uninvited guests would creep into our camp and steal whatever they could lay their hands on and no matter how many sentries were posted.

We were a 'pushover' for them – until the Gurkhas arrived on the scene.

Their commander was Captain Chisholme, whose name I shall always remember. The Gurkhas seemed to worship him and would never let him out of their sight. And they were the boys to deal with the camp thieves. We never had any more night-time visitors.

We plodded on and on. The journey seemed endless, the countryside none too hospitable and we footsore walkers would have given anything for any sort of a train, with or without bandits.

The camel drivers kept a steady slow pace but it was surprising how they ate up the miles and we had a job to keep up with them.

We eventually arrived at Enzeli to find just a few old huts, a couple of houses and a pier sticking out into the Caspian Sea.

The huts were in a terrible state and, getting down to some temporary repairs, we patched up the roofs of two of the buildings with anything we could salvage from the others.

The buildings had apparently been used by Nomads and were in a state which is difficult to describe but we scrubbed them out and generally made them more shipshape.

After our stores had been unloaded, the camels and the Gurkhas with Captain Chisholme set off back whence they had come. We were on our own.

It was my twenty-first birthday and I had no chance to celebrate and nothing to celebrate with. But there I was, in one of the remotest corners of the world, sweet twenty-one and never been kissed – except by a Russian General!

We spent some time at Enzeli. Our job was to build up fortifications in case the Bolsheviks beat Denikin's men and advanced on Persia. We were to set up seashore fortifications with guns transferred from ships left by the Royal Navy.

We had, also, come to repair ships for Denikin's men but a boat arrived with a message that these ships were still in Baku and were in such a state that they could not be sailed to Enzeli.

So, into the boat we went, stores and all, and sailed for Baku. The ships were, indeed, in a sorry state. I don't think the guns had been moved since the Navy left. They hadn't been elevated or trained and were thick with rust.

While I was part of the team which tackled the guns other men worked on the engines and other machinery on board the ships.

We were told off in pairs for our work and I was partnering a chap named Dart in one of the ships when, crunch, the Bolsheviks entered the town and brought work to a halt quicker than a 'wildcat' strike.

Denikin's men fell back in some disorder and there was Stan Smith, quietly working away on the recoil cylinder of one of the guns when, bang, I knew no more.

I had been pretty efficiently thumped over the head and when I woke up I was trussed up like the proverbial chicken. My mates and I were completely immobile, our hands tied behind our backs and our feet lashed tightly together.

The Bolsheviks – fearsome fighting men they seemed – eventually untied our legs and herded us on to the quayside. We were all roped together and marched away under escort.

We entered a grim, bleak room, our hands were untied and we were told to strip naked. Our clothing was searched and our captors, presumably seeking such information as they might find, cut open any double seams.

Only after that did we get our clothes back, to find that our pockets had been emptied so we were left with nothing but the remnants of what we stood up in.

Commander Fraser argued our case with the Astare Nasarate, the head prison guard, for some time but to no avail. We were roped together again and marched off to the prison of Byrloft Chyrma.

It was a humiliating experience because, on either side as we marched, were jeering crowds giving every impression that they were celebrating a great victory.

On our arrival at the prison we were split into two groups and placed in two adjoining cells. With bare walls, no furniture and an earth floor, each cell measured about sixteen foot square at the most and into our cell sixteen people were crammed.

To say that we were uncomfortable is to understate the case. It was utter misery as we endured our first night as prisoners of war.

We were terribly cold and we huddled together for warmth as there were no blankets or bedding of any kind.

We were hungry too, but no food was given to us until about noon the following day. I think it was noon, but our watches had gone and we had no means of being sure of the time. Time was just about the only thing we were going to have plenty of; time to suffer and to watch others suffer even more.

When the food did come it was hardly a slap-up meal but we were ready to eat anything. It consisted of a bowl of soup – they called it soup but it was more like dish water, just about as thick and absolutely tasteless – and half a round of black bread.

This was to be our ration for twenty-four hours. We were still hungry but that, as we were soon to learn, was to be among the least of our troubles.

We had only just scraped the surface of prison life. That first meal was a picnic compared with the reality to come.

# 9 · Hole of Death

What follows is not for the squeamish, but it is a story which must be told, not just because it happened to me but because there are few left now who remember, as I remember, those who lived a living death and died because of the depths to which human beings can be driven in times of war.

It began on that first full day in prison immediately after that first skimpy meal.

We were marched into the courtyard and given ringside seats or standing positions to watch the first massacre.

I suppose there were about forty prisoners, men and women, to be killed and their captors used pretty well every atrocity you could think of and many which you could not bring yourself to think of.

One by one, they slit the women up the middle to about the chest bone, disembowelled them, and left them while they completed their cruel task. Then they shot them as they lay screaming and moaning on the ground.

They made some of the men dip their arms into buckets of acid which was so strong that when the prisoners removed their arms the flesh hung down like huge gauntlets. Time will never erase in my mind the horror of those screams and cries.

We British sailors were forced to watch all this, helpless to do anything about it. Even if you closed your eyes you could never close your ears or your memories to the awful sounds of suffering humanity. It was just the first of many massacres we had to watch and each time we were marched back to our cell to a life which grew more and more grim and ever more hungry.

Suffering is one thing, but watching others suffer, especially your comrades, is, in some ways, even worse. To see man dwindling to skin and bone and scratching on the ground for scraps of food is to know, even in these more comfortable times, something about the world's starvation.

For the early part of our time in prison we had to work. We were

39

lined up each morning in the corridor outside our cell and chained together like a lot of convicts of the old days. Then we were marched through jeering crowds to the railway station where we had to unload sacks of millet from the trucks and carry them to the waiting carts.

This went on until we were so weak that men began to crumble and collapse under the weight of the sacks. Too feeble to work we were of little further use to our captors so, back in the unrelieved misery of our cells, we went on to reduced rations.

For the remainder of our imprisonment our daily diet consisted of a raw fish about the size of a herring and a handful of Barcelona nuts.

We became so hungry that we would have fought amongst ourselves over the food, especially the fish, if it had not been for our Commander. He made us stand back against the cell walls and would call our names, one by one.

When a man's name was called he would rush out, grab a fish and a handful of nuts, and return to the wall to devour them ravenously.

We were allowed out in the courtyard for half-an-hour each day and in that time we had to go to the toilet and get a wash. The toilet! It simply consisted of a hole in the ground with a couple of bricks to put your feet on.

Washing was no easy job either. We had no soap and could only use the grit around the tap to clean our faces and hands a little. In that one half-hour of something like release we would drink enough water to last us until the next day, for that was the only time we saw it.

This daily intake of water made us all pot-bellied and we began to look as if we had been put 'in the family way'.

In times like this simple things assume a great importance. One of these small things which helped to keep us sane was a piece of glass which one of the lads found in the courtyard. We used this to cut our hair away from our eyes and to try, as best we could, to make our bodies a little more comfortable.

But our main preoccupation was to hide this piece of glass for the guards would come in and search the cell at least once a week. They even dug up the earth floor to make it more uncomfortable – but they never did find that piece of glass.

And were we lousy? You bet we were! There were lice in every bit of hair on our bodies, even in our eyebrows, and to make matters worse some of the prison's other occupants would throw packets of lice into the cell through the grid in the door.

We even went round our shirts with our teeth in a vain attempt to kill the eggs which the lice laid in the seams of our clothing.

The first chap to die was a mechanic by the name of Marsh and it was that piece of glass which ended his suffering. He committed suicide, cutting the arteries in his wrists with the glass during the night and lying down to die.

In the morning the guards almost fought over his clothing. They stripped him and left him there in a pool of blood for three or four days until the flies were almost unbearable in the cell.

Four more of my friends were to die before we were released and each time the same thing happened. The body was left where it lay until it almost decomposed.

Outside the prison, the townspeople were not so happy these days for new rules were introduced which made life decidedly less tolerable for them. For instance, the new powers-that-be ordained that in each house there should be only one chair per occupant. All jewellery had to be turned over to the State.

Each person also had to do one voluntary day's work for the State each week and anybody who was absent on this day was shot.

After almost a year of our confinement word went round the prison that a Minister of the Georgian State was to visit the prison.

Georgia, which was holding out against the Bolsheviks, was separated from us by a wide river and the Georgians were defending their bank efficiently enough to stop the Bolsheviks from getting across.

Thus held up, the Bolsheviks resorted to negotiation with the Georgians and we had high hopes that the visit of the Georgian party would give us, at best, a chance of release or, if that failed, at least a slim hope of letting the outside world know we still existed.

When the Georgian Minister arrived he soon discovered that we had, in our party, an interpreter who was also Georgian. His job with us would have been to interpret everything necessary when we arrived at the Caspian Sea.

The Minister immediately negotiated for the interpreter's release and it was only by this lucky chance that we were able to pass a message out for the British Ambassador to tell the outside world that we were still alive.

The message was hidden in a locket which Commander Fraser had somehow managed to conceal from the guards for all those months. The locket contained a picture of his mother.

The Georgian swallowed the locket and some time after his departure his Minister came again to the prison and interviewed our Commander. It was that interview which finally enabled us to say goodbye to that terrible prison.

We were removed to a disused school where the Georgian Minister gave the Commander some Russian roubles with which we were able to buy a little horse flesh and black bread to supplement our diet.

We also got a bar of soap, so we all had a bath, one at a time under the cold water tap in the courtyard – a real treat.

But all this did not have much effect on our lice. We were still lousy for we still wore the clothes in which we had been captured and they were getting more than a bit ragged by now.

After some weeks at the school we were taken out and marched to the station, not in chains this time. It was quite a change. We were put into trucks and away went the train on the first stage of our journey towards freedom.

At the border between Azerbaijan and Georgia we had to walk across a bridge. We were met on the other side by a Colonel Stokes and taken to a real train with carriages.

There was no delay. The train left as soon as we were on board and we were given a very light meal – a quarter of a slice of meat, a little bread and a bar of chocolate.

At every station where we stopped my chum and I tried our best to get some bread, but no luck. We were still under guard and were watched very closely. If we had succeeded I suspect it would have been curtains for the pair of us.

On one occasion we saw Colonel Stokes smoking a cigar. We followed him until he threw the cigar end away, then pounced on it, had a couple of draws each and promptly passed out for the count!

When we arrived at Tiflis, the capital of Georgia, we were taken out of the train and given a complete change of clothing, but we were still lousy. Our old clothes were thrown in a heap and burned.

As the train took us steadily nearer to the comfort of our own people, there was another complete change of clothing and our diet gradually increased until we were on to a full slice of bread and meat at each meal.

When we arrived at Batumi a welcome sight greeted us – a British destroyer. She took us back through the Black Sea to the Bosphorus where we were taken on board the Flagship, HMS *Iron Duke*.

There we were bathed. Our entire bodies were shaved hairless, even our eyebrows, and we were again given fresh clothes, naval clothes this time. Then we went up for a light dinner with the Admiral who thanked us on behalf of the Navy and made a speech.

It was only then that he broke the news that we were not going directly back to England. We were to be the Navy's guests for a Mediterranean cruise on board a sloop, HMS *Heliotrope*, which had been fitted out for us.

The purpose of our cruise was to feed us up and get us strong enough to return to England.

On board the *Heliotrope* our hammocks had already been slung for us and it was not long before we snuggled down in them and enjoyed the best sleep we had had for many months. Special messing arrangements had been made to cater for our tender stomachs and we had a doctor on board.

For the first time I saw myself in a full length mirror down in the bathroom. What a sight – no eyebrows, no hair and a belly that stuck out a mile beneath ribs you could hang your hat on.

But all that was soon to change for we quickly got on to a full diet. We even had the choice of a glass of port wine or a bottle of Guinness with our lunch.

We called at no ports. We just visited isolated bays in different countries and went ashore to play football, to swim or to take any exercise that would help to make us fit and strong.

It was not long before the hair started to grow again on our heads and eyebrows and we began to look a bit more presentable.

Our troubles were not all over though. While we were on the cruise two of our chaps were taken ill. The doctor could do nothing for them so we called in at Malta and they were taken to Bigi Hospital.

We heard later that they had both died – and the irony of their sad end at a time when their ordeal seemed to be over was lost on none of us. There are times when life can be mighty hard.

Their deaths meant that there were now only twelve survivors from the twenty-nine cheerful volunteers who had started out on this stunt.

We eventually set sail for England and arrived at Plymouth to find that we had become celebrities in our absence. But if the Press thought they had a story landing in their laps, they were sadly disappointed.

The reporters were kept away from the ship and we were sworn not to communicate with the Press in any way or to give speeches or lectures about our captivity. All the papers could say was that the men had returned from the 'Black Hole of Baku'.

We dined that evening with the Lord Mayor of Plymouth and his entourage. The following afternoon we went by train to London where we dined with the Minister for Foreign Affairs, Lord Curzon.

It was at this dinner that a rather special presentation ceremony took place. On board the *Heliotrope* we had whipped round to buy a ceremonial sword for Commander Fraser. Properly ordered, the sword was waiting for us when we arrived in England and our Commander graciously received it during dinner with Lord Curzon.

Commander Fraser, who was very proud of that sword, told me afterwards that he used it on all ceremonial occasions. He went onwards and upwards in the Royal Navy and during the Second World War, was Commander-in-Chief of the Home Fleet and was in at the death of the German battleship *Scharnhorst* at the hands of his flagship, HMS *Duke of York*, on 26 December 1943.

In a letter I received from him some time ago, he told me that we were the only living survivors of the 'Black Hole of Baku'. Now, alas, I am the only one, having lost Sir Bruce Fraser in 1981.

# 10 · The B(u)oy Jumper

It was wonderful to be home again and free to make sure that the back pay bulging my pockets did not stay there long. Money had meant little in the life or death struggle I had just been through in the 'Black Hole of Baku' but now it meant the chance to let my hair down and enjoy myself. After all, it was also something of a new experience to have some hair to let down!

I learned from my mother that Lady Fraser had written individually to the families of all her son's men telling them not to give up hope, even though we had all been reported missing, believed killed. In addition, she had put each family in touch with another that was not too far distant and they had been able to share their troubles.

In these ways, Lady Fraser had done much to keep hope alive among the people who might otherwise have given us up for lost and that hope had been fulfilled with our return from the dead. With these Christian acts of kindness, the Commander's mother had shown her own concern and drawn our families into that deep sense of comradeship which had held the survivors of Baku together.

All good things come to an end and my leave was over all too soon. The Navy, like the sea itself, rolls forward with little more than a backward glance to past events, even after two years of captivity.

For me, the one backward glance came when we were issued with our First World War medals. Mine consisted of the 1914–15 Star, the General Service and Victory Medals. To be honest, these medals became something of an embarrassment while we were in Chatham Barracks because, every three or four months, the powers-that-be would change the way in which we had to wear them.

First, they had to be strung on a long bar. That was not suitable so they had then to be overlapped on a smaller bar. Then the ribbons had to be three inches long. Then they were altered back to two and a half inches.

Every time the rules were changed we had to take the medals to the tailors, and, by the time the Navy had made up its mind about this apparently important question of high policy, the alterations had cost us a good deal of hard earned cash.

We had to wear the medals all day on Sundays and on all ceremonial occasions, but far from glowing with pride in them, we began to regard them as a perishing nuisance.

No mention was made on my papers of the 5th Order of St George, which I received from that affectionate Russian General in the Black Sea. This neither surprised nor disappointed me in the slightest because it meant that no awkward questions were likely to be asked as to the whereabouts of my Russian 'gong'.

However much I came to dislike my First World War medals, I do not recall that I ever actually tied up a spud net with any of them, so they must have meant something to me, I suppose!

Having been made a range finder, second class, at Gunnery School, I went back to sea on board HMS *McKay*, a destroyer leader with five 4.7-inch guns, one 3-inch anti-aircraft gun and a couple of pom-poms. She was also fitted with depth charges on rails which she would drop at speed – and she could do 35 knots!

The *McKay* was under the command of one Captain Moore, a Scotsman, a brilliant seaman and a stickler for discipline. He could manoeuvre the ship much like a yachtsman would handle a sailing boat and he believed that everything should be done at speed. Every member of the ship's company had to be right on top of his job and there was no room for anybody who couldn't match up to the Skipper's own high standards.

I was fo'c'stle man and as 'buoy jumper' my job was to tie the ship up to a buoy when we came into harbour. The normal procedure of lowering a boat for the buoy jumper was too slow for Captain Moore. Instead I had to stand on a fender which was lowered from the bow with a lifeline crowfooted to my jacket, the pockets of which contained a punch, a hammer and pellets of lead to fix a shackle securely to the buoy.

The captain would steam the ship up to the buoy, touch it with the bow, and I had to jump. That jump on to the buoy had to be timed to perfection if I was not to land in the water or between ship and buoy.

First I had to fix the wire, then they would haul the cable out to me so that I could fix the Munroe shackle and secure the vessel to the buoy.

Though I say it myself, I did get quite proficient at this athletic job and could well have become one of the best jumpers in the Fleet. I knew, as we all did, that if the job was not done properly I was for the 'high jump' anyway!

The Skipper's renowned seamanship really came into its own one day when we entered the narrow little harbour of Aberdeen which had a number of locks. He drove the ship stern first through the locks at about 20 knots and the local fishermen stood agape as he brought her up alongside. As I sit here now I bet he wouldn't have cracked an egg as the ship drew alongside the quay.

We were based at Port Edgar in Scotland and at every opportunity I would travel the dozen or so miles to Edinburgh where, true to the sailor's tradition, I met a girl. She was lovely and I became rather sweet on her. But the budding romance was destined to be short-lived.

One day, as I returned on board, the coxswain hailed me. 'You've got to go and see the Skipper this morning; you're in Captain's Report' he told me with that totally unnecessary hint of glee which coxswains and the like seemed to have when they were giving you bad news!

Up to the Captain I went, off cap, stand to attention. Sternly, he said, 'I told you a month ago to pass for Leading Seaman. You haven't done so, therefore I am stopping your leave until you have been into barracks here in Port Edgar and passed.'

It was no use protesting. My chances of romance with a Scottish lass were well and truly nipped in the bud and, reluctantly, I went into barracks to pass for Leading Seaman.

The end of my romance pretty well coincided with our departure from Scotland for a cruise in the Baltic during which we were to have further evidence of Captain Moore's belief that discipline and efficiency was demanded from everybody, including Royalty.

The newest recruit to our ship's company was Prince George who, to be entirely polite, appeared to us hardened old salts as a man of slight stature and considerable vulnerability to sea sickness. In fact, he seemed to be sea sick as soon as we rattled the cable on the fo'c'stle ready to weigh anchor.

But our strict, seamanlike Captain held that the *McKay* carried no passengers, Royal or otherwise, and Prince George was excused nothing.

One day the Prince was told off to take the postman ashore in the skiff. The problem was that he could not pull sculls. The Captain's answer was to put him in the skiff with the cook's ladle as an implement with which to practise. Watching him as he struggled to master the art, you couldn't help feeling it was a hard way to learn a lesson in seamanship. But that was the way of Captain Moore. You had to learn the lesson – and you had to remember it.

I became the Prince's escort, accompanying him on shore to the various official functions he attended in the ports of Norway and Sweden as we toured the Baltic. This glimpse of the high life as a Royal escort did not last long for the Prince fell sick and was transferred ashore to hospital where, we were told, appendix trouble was diagnosed. He later became Duke of Kent.

To my knowledge, Captain Moore was never promoted, but I hesitate to guess whether this was, in any way, the result of his handling of our Royal sailor.

Meanwhile, the Navy was gradually changing and education was becoming more important than ever; more important, some might believe, than seamanship itself.

Machinery, guns and instruments were becoming more sophisticated and the sailor had to be fairly well educated to cope with them. There were men on board who couldn't write their names and who believed that this was far less necessary to a sailor than the skills involved in splicing a rope or pulling a skiff.

One old sailor, for example, was the bosun's right-hand man. He could do anything in the seamanship line but he could not write. In fact, I used to write his letters home for him.

It was at that time that an educational test was introduced for all Leading Seamen and those who could not pass it were de-rated to Able seamen. Many good men, including the bosun's right-hand man, were unable to clear this new hurdle; men who had gained their knowledge of the sea, not through theory, but in the hardest school of all during years of practical experience in all weathers and in war as well as peace.

The time I had spent at the Grammar School back in Great Yarmouth now had its value as I passed the test. I was confirmed as a Leading Seaman and put second-in-charge of the fo'c'stle until the *McKay* eventually paid off and I went back to barracks.

# 11 · Eruptions

Since, at that time, dry land gave me itchy feet, I was glad to be soon leaving barracks to resume my flirtation with destroyers. I was on draft, in fact, to HMS *Montrose*, a destroyer leader similar in all respects to the *McKay*, except that she was stationed in the Mediterranean.

For a time we cruised the Med. uneventfully, enjoying welcome bouts of leave at Malta. But you must have noticed how, even when there are no actual wars going on, the world is always full of local squabbles. Somebody, somewhere is always trying to stand up for what he sees as his rights.

In our time in the Med. there were one or two trouble spots, notably at Port Said. As ever, we were not very well informed on the reasons for the riots, but riots there were and it was our job to guard the dockyard.

We somehow had to hold the mob back by forming a long line and carrying bayonets fixed to loaded rifles which we were not allowed to fire. We had to stand our ground as the mob approached and spat in our faces.

Or, by way of variation in their tactics, the rioters would retreat only to throw bricks, rotten fruit and other unmentionable missiles at us.

We were not allowed to retaliate in any way – not allowed, that is, until Lord Louis Mountbatten, at that time the Captain of the fleet, came out to see how the affair was going. His prompt reaction was to give us the opportunity to make a charge.

We were armed, not with rifles, but with axe helves which had a thong on one end that you could wrap round your wrist and a lead bored into the other. They made quite handy weapons.

On the day of the charge, the guard lined up as usual, carrying rifles. But this time things were different for we lined up behind the guard and, at a given order, broke through their ranks wielding our axe helves to good effect.

The surprised crowd fell back as the implements did their work and I'm afraid I have to admit that I must have cracked a few skulls that day. Anyway, from then on, the people kept their distance and never again interfered with the guard.

But such is the unpredictable nature of a varied life in the Royal Navy that you might spend one week clouting the local population over the head with an axe helve and the next helping them to survive a natural disaster.

The 'riot police' of Port Said became angels of mercy on the island of Sicily after Mt Etna had erupted. In front of the oncoming lava the Sicilians stood, held crosses and prayed for deliverance.

You could say that we were the answer to their prayers. We immediately set to work. One party of sailors filled sandbags on the beach while the rest of us, stationed on a slight incline down to the nearby town, built a wall of sandbags in the form of an arrow head to divert the lava away on both sides.

We worked in tremendous heat as the great flow of seemingly irresistible lava steadily approached and eventually hit our makeshift wall. So great was the inexorable force of the lava as it built up against our defences that some of it started to flow over the top of the wall.

We watched helplessly as, in places, the wall seemed to stagger under the strain. But, suddenly, the great flow of hot lava began to divide and flow down on either side of our sandbag wall towards the vineyards in the valleys below. It was preferable to sacrifice these than to see the lava engulfing the town.

In places our wall was breached and some of the lava flowed through to the outskirts of the town, destroying one or two houses, but our makeshift wall had stood the test and the Sicilian people breathed a huge sigh of relief. Etna had stopped erupting and the bulk of their town had been saved by the Royal Navy.

We put up tents for the homeless and arranged food supplies and medical attention. In response, the grateful Sicilians, always ready for a party, invited us to a fiesta full of feasting, singing, dancing, plenty of wine and some hefty pats on the back.

Sailors, who had so recently been spat on and attacked by crowds, were now mobbed by friends and what a pleasant memory it was as we set sail for Malta with the music and thanks of the jubilant Sicilians still ringing in our ears.

But there was another bad time in store for us when we were sent to help the people of two islands off Greece where there had been an earthquake. It seemed to us that the people around the beautiful

Mediterranean lived in almost daily fear of some natural disaster or other and we could do little more than dig out the dead from the rubble of their homes, arrange food supplies and tents and make the survivors as comfortable as possible.

Eventually, when the ship paid off and we headed back to Chatham, we could reflect that it had been a good Commission in HMS *Montrose* with some excitement, plenty of action and very few dull moments.

Six months later, after a spell with the Home Fleet, I was sailing back to the Med. in my new ship HMS *Broke*, yet another destroyer leader, and at this point it might be helpful to give an insight into the messing arrangements on board a destroyer in the 1920s.

The mess deck was in the forward part of the ship, stretching from the bridge to the bow. When the ship was commissioned each sailor was allotted to one of four messes on the main deck. The stokers occupied the next deck down, their 'home' in the bilges being approached through a watertight hatch and a circular hatch in the seamen's mess deck.

Our messes actually consisted of four tables, each accommodating sixteen men with a Leading Seaman in charge. Standard rations for each man were half a pound of meat, a pound of bread and half a pound of potatoes per day.

To supplement this pretty basic grub provided by the Navy, the Leading Seaman was issued with a canteen chit book. These chits were our 'currency' with which the cooks of the mess, detailed by the Leading Seaman, used to pay for extra food either when the canteen boat came alongside or from the ship's purser or victualling staff.

There were strict limitations, however, on the amount to which a Leading Seaman could supplement the diet of his mess by using these chits. If he used more than he was allowed, the Navy deducted the difference out of his pocket money. If he underspent – and, to be sure, that happened very rarely – he got a refund which he shared with his men.

The rations and the lack of time allowed for the preparation of meals hardly encouraged good cooks to produce high quality food. It may not have been delicate but it was substantial and satisfying and it was amazing what men could produce with so few resources.

Normally, the Leading Seaman would detail one senior Able Seaman as cook of the mess with a junior seaman to help. They would draw their potatoes from the spud locker, meat from the butcher and bread from the baker. Then, back in the mess in the evening, they would have to peel the spuds and prepare the food for dinner the following day since no time was allowed in the morning for these jobs.

In fact, the cooks of the messes had to prepare the dinner in the ten minutes free time which was allowed during 'stand easy' at about 10.30 am.

If the cook of the mess had decided on a pie, he would have cut the meat up and put it in a dish the previous evening. Then, during 'stand easy', he would rush down to the mess and put the pastry on; 'spreading an awning on the meat' we called it. Then he would rush the finished job up to the galley for cooking.

The spuds also had to go up to the galley, in a dish if they were to be baked or in a net if boiled spuds were on the menu. It was all a bit of a scramble to get these manoeuvres completed in just ten minutes.

But the duties of cook of the mess did not end there. He and his junior also had to wash up after breakfast, dinner, tea and supper and were allowed half-an-hour in the morning to scrub out the mess.

Despite all this, we tucked into some substantial and traditional Navy dishes. For example, a 'schooner on the rocks' comprised potatoes put in a dish with the joint of meat on top and baked. A 'three-decker' occupied a large pot in which two great dollops of meat and vegetables were separated by layers of 'duff'(pastry).

The cook of the mess could make his own choice of what to serve for 'afters' but here again there was very little room for imaginative concoctions. If he couldn't spell tapioca on the mess chit he would invariably write 'rize' (rice).

If the food was pretty basic in destroyers, the sanitary arrangements were no less primitive than they had been in my first ship, the *Orion*.

There were no bathrooms and we again found ourselves doing the Long John Silver act in a bucket, getting one leg in first to wash one side of the body and then doing the other half.

Certainly, life on board destroyers lacked many of the refinements of civilisation, but this could be one of the reasons why the little ships were sailed by a rather special breed of hard living men, ever ready for a bit of action to relieve the monotony and, when the chips were down, held together by a fierce bond of loyalty to their comrades and their ship.

# 12 · Amazon Adventure

Remember what I said about volunteering? Well, Juggins here went and did it again; and this time it sent me literally right up the creek without a paddle and a very big creek it was, too.

A signal had been received asking for volunteers to go into the Brazilian jungle in search of one Colonel Fawcett, an explorer who had gone missing. The Colonel's fate was the subject of a lot of speculation by the newspapers back home. Had he been captured by a tribe of Amazon Indians? Was he a prisoner in the depths of the jungle? Had he been kidnapped and made king of some native tribe? Nobody knew, so the Navy decided to send in a party to try and locate the Colonel, if at all possible, and unravel the mystery.

I was one of the twelve volunteers who were accepted and placed under the command of a Lieutenant Bradley, a very nice chap. We set sail for the Amazon and went up the great South American river as far as we could by ship, reaching Bara, a city which was the centre of the rubber trade.

It was a thriving industrial city with trams, cabarets and dance halls. The rubber was brought in from the jungle and heated up to be made into huge balls or squares which were loaded on to ships for export to many countries.

There was no sign of the desolation which was to befall Bara after the rubber boom evaporated. When I saw the city fifteen years later it was absolutely deserted.

The cranes had fallen down and the jungle was growing up in the streets and through the tramcars. This had been the impact of developments in manufacture of synthetic rubber and the rubber trees had outlived their usefulness. But Bara was still a bustling city at the time of our Amazon expedition and there we were kitted out.

Our gear consisted of khaki shorts and jacket. All our personal necessities were to be carried in packs on our backs. We were issued with rifles and ammunition and each of us also carried a large sharp Bowie knife at our belt.

Porters were recruited to accompany us to carry the stores and the trade goods which we were to distribute in friendly villages in exchange for a safe passage or information about Colonel Fawcett.

Thus equipped, we plunged deeper into the South American jungles, paddling on up the river in canoe-shaped boats as far as we could. I think we travelled by water for three days until we reached some falls which we could not negotiate.

There was nothing for it but to hit the trail on foot so we hauled the boats up into the bush, camouflaged them with branches and undergrowth and, with the porters well loaded, headed off into the jungle.

Led by a guide who was supposed to deal with the natives for us, we slogged on and on. At times we had to hack our way through the jungle, it was so dense.

Thankfully, when we came to a village, the natives were friendly. Our Lieutenant had a good long talk with the Chief and gave him and some of his followers some of the trade goods we had brought with us, strings of cheap beads (probably from Woolworths), little mirrors, other bright objects and knives.

We carried on for days. Sometimes we would only make about a mile in a day as we had to hack our way through the jungle and the interlacing vines which hung like heavy lace curtains all about us. It was hot, humid, green and suffocating. At each village we asked for news of Colonel Fawcett but, even where the villagers were friendly, there was none.

As we plunged ever deeper into the jungle a gradual change came over the natives we met. At each village we reached the reception was less and less friendly until we began to find 'ghost' villages totally deserted yet with signs of recent habitation.

The local population had known we were coming and we felt the unnerving experience of being watched by hundreds of unseen eyes from the jungle all around.

Even so, we would still leave small gifts at some point in the middle of the village, hoping they would find them after we had gone and realise that we were trying to be friendly.

Shy though they obviously were – more scared, perhaps, even than us – the natives nevertheless showed no sign of hostility and we tramped on into the forest.

We passed the remains of several old Inca settlements, ancient towns which to this day are still being discovered. But we had no time to explore.

One day we came to a clearing in sight of one of these Inca villages and we made camp. During the evening we were attacked by pygmies using blow pipes. These natives were far from friendly and we opened fire on them. Whether or not we hit any we did not know but the noise of the guns probably scared them away.

One of our chaps, however, had been hit in the shoulder by a dart. We gave him what first aid treatment we could and tried to suck the poison out of the wound, but he gradually became worse.

There was no alternative but to send him back to Bara with one of our party and two of the bearers. We made a rough stretcher from boughs and vines and set them off to follow our trail back as quickly as they could.

That was the last we saw of any of them. We never heard anything more of our wounded comrade; whether the group was killed or whether they simply got lost and starved to death we were never to know.

In any case, we soon had our own problems. Immediately after the attack by the pygmies all our bearers deserted us. They simply crept out at night and we awoke in the morning to find no trace of them.

We could not carry on much further transporting all our stores and food so we discarded some of the extra clothing and food, packed it all up carefully and hid it in the bush. Then, carrying just the minimum of food for survival and just such clothes as we wore, we set out again, travelling light.

We tramped on for two days. Food was getting very short. Then we came to a very swampy patch of jungle.

We were absolutely pestered by mosquitos, swarms of them. They had been plaguing us all the way through the jungle but never before in these numbers. It was a sweating, stinging infested sump of the world which, as if mosquitos were not penance enough, was also populated by leeches. They clung to our legs, slimy, fat, repugnant blood suckers and we had to pull hard to get them off.

So we had a consultation. If Colonel Fawcett had come within a hundred miles of this God-forsaken place we might never have known, anyway. What hope had we of finding him? More chance, it seemed, of perishing in the attempt. In short, we felt we had reached the end of the road. We had done our bit and nobody could expect more.

So we did an about turn and began the long hard slog to pick our way back through the jungle the way we had come.

On reaching the clearing where we had left our stores, we had a jolly good meal of corned beef and biscuits, packed some more food into our haversacks and continued the search for our homeward trail.

The going was fairly easy and we made much better time going back than we had on the outward journey for the trail was still clear and we had marker trees to guide us.

We eventually got back to the boats. Mercifully, they were intact. We uncovered them but we had nobody to paddle them so we made ourselves some rough paddles from the jungle and launched one boat and towed the other.

The tide was with us so we made fairly good progress although our paddling was none too seamanlike and our craft not exactly manoeuvrable and we were weaker.

At one of the friendliest villages, however, we soon had more than enough volunteer paddlers; so many, in fact, that we had to select our crews from among them.

Thus, we arrived back at Bara. We had tried but failed and we had come back with a totally different crew from that which had accompanied us into the jungle.

There was time for a run ashore, some onion beer and a few smokes before we returned to the ship. Our Amazon adventure was over and, without delay, I found myself back aboard HMS *Broke* at Malta.

The remainder of the Commission was happy-go-lucky. We had a great crew and a fine ship under us and we had a marvellous time visiting the ports around the Mediterranean and enjoying Malta, our home base.

One night, I remember, three of us went ashore to the White Ensign Club and I won the tombola; a magnificent £21. We picked up three Janes in the town, hired a garry, a horse-drawn carriage, and went out to Booji-Booji to Peter Dowell Hotel.

There we had a slap-up dinner and went midnight bathing and we were drinking until the early hours of the morning. Back at the *Broke* it was us three who were broke and we had to borrow the money to pay our fare in the diso (boat).

This was just one of the happy incidents which have always helped me to remember that Commission with affection. At least we had succeeded in forgetting those pygmies and their blow pipes and the mosquitos – and those bloody leeches!

# 13 · *Ramillies* and the Apes

The Royal Navy, for most of the first half of the twentieth century, was the Navy of Big Guns; and I don't just mean Admirals! And the guns were biggest in battleships like the *Ramillies*, a famous name even now wherever the Navy men meet.

Having been recommended to go in for Gunnery Instructor, while still serving in HMS *Broke*, I found myself heading back to Gunnery School – only to be told I was too young and lacked experience.

Young I might have been, but I reckon I had picked up more experience than some of the instructors. Anyway, the fact that I was not officially qualified did not stop me from doing the job of an instructor for a time. I had to take young officers on the parade ground first thing in the morning for rifle drill. I also took classes during the day.

Until, that is, a draft came up again for me – to the *Ramillies*. A fine battleship, she toted more guns than all the Western gunslingers in history – eight 15-inch, a whole armoury of 6-inch and, for good measure, a small battery of four anti-aircraft guns.

I became range-finder and my domain was in just about the most exposed part of the ship, in the foretop right at the top of the foremast. I was also made captain-in-charge of the boat deck and was responsible for more than thirty men.

We arrived at Plymouth where the ship was commissioned. Then we went out on navigation trials, gun trials, compass swinging and all the work-up routine for a new crew.

Then back to Plymouth and just for a change, we were set to paint the ship a lighter shade of grey. The reason for this special bit of spit and polish was that we were to be King's Ship during the sailing programme of Cowes Week. But painting that ship was to claim two lives.

To paint the topmast and the mainmast underneath we had to rig a net for the sailors to scramble into. Painting underneath the tops was a tricky and arduous job for two able seamen with a Petty Officer in charge. The net had to be securely rigged but, unknown to us, a rope was chafing on the sharp edge of an angle iron. Suddenly it gave way, shooting all three of them out of the net.

Many feet above the deck one able seaman managed to grab a shroud as he fell. It must be pretty unusual for a shroud to save a man's life; but it did, even though the man's arms were nearly pulled out of their sockets.

Sadly, the other two were not so lucky. They plunged to the iron boat deck and were killed instantly. It was a bad start to our Commission.

After that, every time we painted ship during that Commission, it was my job to take charge of a special band of men to paint the foremast and I had to rig up nets with wire lashings so that they didn't chafe through.

As guard ship at Cowes we had a grandstand view of the races. Our Commander had a small private yacht of his own and competed in some of the events for smaller craft. I crewed for him and, at times, he would let me take the helm, so I began to get a taste for sailing.

After Cowes we went back to Plymouth, repainted the ship its customary dark shade of grey and were then diverted to Malta where we became one of the Mediterranean Fleet.

A bizarre period of my life at sea followed. We were sent to the West Coast of Africa to test conditions for the crew in a battleship in tropical weather – and it was awful. Dressed only in shorts we were soaked in sweat all day long.

About a dozen of us, including Juggins here, were chosen for an even hotter torture, testing a new type of gas mask.

We had to do all sorts of arduous and strenuous jobs with the masks on. After loading about twenty rounds into the 6-inch guns or pulling the oars of the cutter for three miles, your mask filled with sweat and you were in danger of choking on it.

Whether or not the mask was a success we never knew but just thanked our lucky stars when we saw the last of it.

There were the lighter moments, of course, the fun ashore for instance, at Accra, along the Gold and Ivory Coasts and in Sierre Leone where we stayed for some time, even though it was then known as the white man's grave.

We would walk up the hill to the barracks occupied by the Army, because it was the only place where we could get a drop of beer and they would give us our lunch.

But even food was not eaten without some snags. You had to get your meal from the cookhouse and walk with it on a tray across to the dining room. As you walked you ran the gauntlet of the vultures which would dive down on you and pinch the choicest bits from your plate.

This gave the watching soldiers a good laugh. They were used to this and foiled the vultures by putting a plate over their food.

We also went bathing in a bay that was netted off against sharks. We moored our boat outside the nets, scrambled across the rocks to the shore, stripped off and were larking around in the water when a couple of rock apes came down the foreshore to inspect our clothing.

We rushed up the beach and chased them away, but back they came; this time about a dozen of them, chattering, banging their chests in true King Kong style and making all sorts of weird noises.

Again we chased them away, and again they returned. A whole herd of them advanced down the beach and, there being safety in numbers, they wouldn't retreat.

There was no chasing this lot away. Instead, they came right down to the water's edge and tore our clothing to shreds.

It doesn't happen often, but there are just the rare occasions when the Navy has to retreat, and this was one of them. We crawled out along the rocks and into the boat, returning to the ship in our bathing suits and somewhat to the amusement of the company.

On our way back to the Mediterranean base we got caught on the edge of a cloudburst and had to clear the upper deck.

It didn't wait to rain; the heavens simply opened and out came God's bathwater. Just a solid sheet of water and there was hail, too, stones as big as florins (10p pieces to you) and they did quite a lot of damage. They tore the awning and went right through the wings of a light aircraft that we had on top of B turret. I have never seen a storm like it, before or since.

I was cox'n of the second cutter. She was a 32ft clinker-built 12-oared cutter, sloop rigged, and I soon found that she was quite a good sailing boat.

We entered several local races, coming second or third. She just seemed to lack that little something extra that would give her first place; but I couldn't figure out what it was.

Then we decided to replace the sail on the boom, putting the strop on the boom a foot lower towards the base of the mast.

We also fitted a block and tackle at the foot of the sail where it was normally fixed by a round hook down to a strop in the bottom of the boat. We could now pull the sail almost vertical and this was a great help because, in a sloop-rigged cutter you had to dip the boom right round the mast on each tack you made.

We also fixed the drop keel so it would go down another foot. This made quite a difference because in a strong breeze we could continue with full sail instead of taking in a reef.

From then on we won every race we entered, including the Combined Fleets Iron Duke Cup and several other Combined Fleet races. She was a lovely boat.

In these races you had to have your full equipment aboard; two beakers of water, twelve oars, two boat hooks, anchor and cable, a sailmaker's pack consisting of a palm and needle, sailmaker's twine and lump of wax also the repair pack with its copper plates, canvas, tallow and copper tacks ready to repair a hole in your boat.

After a race competitors had to go alongside the Flagship and I have seen boats disqualified for not having a simple thing like a palm and needle aboard.

We spent many a pleasant hour sailing. Whenever we had a bit of spare time I would ask the Commander if I could lower the cutter and go sailing and invariably he agreed for he was a great sailing man. Mind you, I was undiplomatic enough once to beat him in a race but he accepted defeat with good grace and gave us a bottle of beer down in the wardroom.

After exercises with the Combined Fleet we would spend a few days at Gibraltar where we would have a good time. We used to smuggle ourselves across to Langolene, which was out of bounds. We also went up to the peak; as if we hadn't seen enough of apes!

Our favourite drink on shore was coffee royal. This consisted of a cup of coffee containing two or three lumps of sugar and a tot of rum. It cost tuppence ha'penny!

After a few of these we used to come on board quite merry and it was on one such night – round about midnight – that a group of us decided to take Old Dick on board our ship.

Old Dick was a horse that had formerly been employed by the dockyard. But he was old. He had been paid off and was living a life of freedom in retirement. He simply wandered around the dockyard every day making friends with any sailor who would give him a bit of bread, a lump of sugar or some other tit-bit.

Cautiously, we opened the stable door and gave Old Dick a couple of lumps of sugar. That was enough. He followed us along the mole and we got him up the gangway and on deck.

Unfortunately, the Officer of the Watch was doing his rounds and we got caught. We were all put into the Captain's report. Thank heavens, he was a lenient man and saw the funny side of our little escapade. We got off with seven days' leave stopped.

But the funniest part of the story came the next morning. There was no way to get Old Dick off the ship under his own steam. They had to get the entire port watch to rig a derrick; the sailmaker had to make a body belt and sling and it was quite a job to get the old horse up, over the side and down on to the mole.

Old Dick was a character that many a sailor from my time at sea will probably remember; the dockyard horse who boarded the *Ramillies* and got a lift out of life.

During the *Ramillies* commission I was ordered to qualify for Petty Officer and recommended for Gunnery Instructor. After the ship paid off. I went back to Chatham and so, for me, the commission ended where it had begun.

This time, however, I was considered neither too young nor too inexperienced. I qualified as Gunnery Instructor and from then on took classes right through to seaman gunner.

But the next instalment of my story was already creeping up on me. I didn't know it, but I was China-bound.

# 14 · Pirates, Geishas and a Straw Hat

HMS *Cumberland*, due to go out to China, was the ship which would give young Stan his first taste of the mystic East, Geisha girls and all.

The ship was a 10,000-ton conventional cruiser with eight 8-inch guns and quite a battery of anti-aircraft guns. She had a cruising capacity of 10,400 miles without refuelling.

My job was in the director tower which was at the top of the ship and had two telescopes. I was supposed to sight the target through the telescopes and as I moved them up or down or to the left or right, so they moved indicators in all the gun turrets.

All the gun-layers and trainers had to do was to follow a small red pointer and keep their own pointer in line.

It was my responsibility – and quite a nice one, I must admit – to fire the guns with a trigger in the director tower.

We set sail from Plymouth, went through the Mediterranean, the Suez Canal and the Red Sea and, after calling at Colombo, finally put into Hong Kong.

As might well be imagined by now, Stan and his mates had a pretty good time ashore in the Crown Colony. We soon got accustomed to the Chinese ways of bargaining and the currency.

We were paid in Chinese dollars at a set rate to the pound, I think it was about twenty. However, the dollar on shore used to fluctuate quite a lot.

When we got paid on the first of the month we would take our money to the bank on shore, changing it into pounds when the dollar was high and back when it was low. In this way it was possible to save a month's pay and spend a month's pay in one month.

Alas, this little ruse did not last very long, for the Governor of the Bank of England came out to Hong Kong – his name was Montague Norman – and he levelled off the dollar so that it only fluctuated a few cents each way.

At this time there was another official decision which affected the lives of some of our people though not all were too keen to admit they noticed! The Governor decided to close down the official brothels!

It must be said that these had been well run. They had been inspected by the ship's doctors periodically and were kept clean and relatively healthy.

The decision to close them inevitably threw all the girls on to the streets, so that you could hardly walk a few yards without being accosted by a young Chinese girl offering her favours for a small fee.

According to the custom of the country then – and quite possibly now – a man who got into debt would have to rely on his daughters, if he had any, to pay it off. They were expected to continue as prostitutes until Dad's debt was cleared.

Our own doctors had a favourite saying, if you went sick with some small ailment like boils or pimples, 'Go ashore and get a woman'.

Instead of that, we went to sea to get ourselves some pirates. Pirate patrol – on which the *Cumberland* was sent – had to be quite a regular practice because the pirates were numerous in the waters around Hong Kong. Thick as thieves, you might say.

They sailed old junks in which they would conceal an ancient gun – usually a muzzle-loading cannon. This antiquated weapon was, more often than not, loaded with all manner of scrap iron, grape shot by courtesy of some Chinese Steptoe, no doubt.

The pirates would approach a merchant or passenger ship and suddenly the innocent looking old junk would erupt with a shot from the gun. Then the victims would be held up for ransom, their ship looted, and the pirates would make good their escape.

The principle was much the same as the old Q-ships that I had served in a few years before, but I couldn't help feeling that the motive was rather different and the victims more defenceless.

In no way could we claim our mission was a success. To be honest, we never actually found any pirates, although we stopped several dhows while on the patrol. However, before going back to harbour we got orders to raid a pirate village in Bias Bay.

To get to the village we were landed in boats on the beach. From there we had to wade waist deep through paddy fields with our rifles held above our heads. When we got to the village it was deserted, just the presence of a few scavenging dogs making the place seem even more empty and desolate.

Our search of the village revealed one hut containing evidence that pirates lived there – civilian clothes, a couple of wrist watches, cigarette cases and other indications that this was one of their hide-outs.

We sent patrols into the hills around the village but no sign of life could they find. So, when they came back, we simply set fire to the village – to teach the pirates a lesson – waded back through the paddy fields and returned on board ship.

It was not until submarines were used on pirate patrols that the success rate against this wily and elusive quarry began to rise. The submarines could keep watch at periscope depth and, as soon as they were sure a vessel was a pirate ship, they would surface and a couple of rounds would sink her. Gradually the submarines put paid to the piracy.

From Hong Kong we went up to Wei Hi Wei, which was a naval base in Northern China. There was quite a large deep water bay in which the ship could manoeuvre for gunnery practice and other exercises.

On shore there was just a small village and a large naval canteen. The latter sold English beer and the tables were piled high with peanuts, so our staple diet on shore became beer and peanuts.

There was also a restaurant where the menu included spring chickens – small chickens which were sold for ten to fifteen cents each, about a shilling in our money.

We stayed there for some time, doing gunnery or torpedo practice and all the necessary exercises which go towards working a crew into a new ship. That done satisfactorily, we set sail for a cruise to Japan.

We called at several small places and finished up at Nagasaki where three of us applied for leave and were given four days. So off we went to the capital, Tokyo, and from there on to the hot springs.

Not far from these was a lovely, typically Japanese hotel. We had to leave our shoes in the hall and enter the hotel proper in our stockinged feet. There, we three British sailors, all wide-eyed and wondering, were met by the hotel manager, who bowed his introduction and welcome to us and promised every attention during our stay.

He told us that a Geisha girl would be detailed to each one of us and that our every need was her command – except, of course, any needs which might occur to us while we were in bed! This was definitely a no go area for the Geishas!

But we were soon to find that a man can have an awful lot of needs attended to by a good Geisha before he ever gets tired enough to snuggle between the sheets.

The first item on the agenda was a bath. Our Geisha girls first removed all our clothes and then directed us to get into a tub under which burned a small fire.

Steadily, they stoked the fire, gradually the temperature of the water in the tub rose. Boy, did we have red faces!

The contrast from almost boiling water to a cold shower gave us goose pimples on our goose pimples and effectively ensured that our relationship with the Geishas remained entirely platonic.

We felt just about ready for a marble slab, and that was exactly where we went next for a massage carried out with sweet smelling oils.

Duly massaged and smelling more sweetly than most sailors should after a spell at sea, we were each draped in a Japanese robe and ushered down to the dining room for a real oriental dinner. The wine tasted good, but it was pretty potent and that ensured, as time went by, that we hardly knew, or cared, what we were eating.

I seem to recall that we started off with birds' nest soup and finished with sharks' fins and bamboo shoots. Whatever the menu, however, we really enjoyed the meal.

The Geisha girls showed us how to use chopsticks and we got on quite well with them. In fact, they waited on us hand and foot, tending to our smallest comforts and even lighting our cigarettes for us. We did not have to lift a finger to help ourselves.

After dinner we adjourned to the lounge where the Geisha girls entertained us by playing mandolins, dancing and singing – in Japanese, of course – and then it was time for sleep.

The Geishas escorted us to our bedrooms, undressed us and put us to bed, just as if we were children. Then they left, just as if we were children!

In the morning they returned, each bearing a cup of tea. They also brought us our uniforms which had been washed, starched and pressed while we had been living our life of luxury.

Breakfast awaited us in the dining room and after we had eaten our personal Geishas bowed us out of the door and we went, all sparkling clean and refreshed, back to our ship.

It was the sort of interesting short leave I shall never forget for I enjoyed every minute of it in a Japan still steeped in its old traditions and customs and yet to take up arms against us.

In fact, the Japanese had some very quaint customs and we were learning more and more about them every day. In the evenings, as we wandered through the cobbled streets of Nagasaki, oriental lanterns swung outside the picturesque shops.

The lanterns, small and delicate and made of papier mache, were filled with glow worms which gave a surprising amount of light.

But Nagasaki also holds memories for me of a different sort, for it was my turn to shine one morning when we were returning to the ship after a night ashore.

A group of us was waiting on the jetty for the boat and we were watching a kind of free circus show. Long poles extended from the jetty with a triangular net suspended under them. At the end of one of the poles was a platform from which the net was lowered or hauled in as soon as the fish appeared above it.

We saw a Japanese fisherman run out along this pole, with no apparent effort at all and dart up into his little nest over the fishing net.

Needless to say, some imaginative soul dared me to have a go. Again, needless to say, I agreed. After all, I was still full of bravado with a few drinks inside me and, anyway, I never could resist a dare.

Well, there are no prizes for guessing what happened to yours truly. Sober, I was no more sure-footed than anybody else used to a life at sea. Drunk, I was full of confidence and athleticism but a little short on balance. Mind you, I did get half way along the pole before I fell in.

Perhaps those swimming lessons in that canvas suit way back at Shotley had been designed to prepare adventurous matelots for just such a catastrophe as this, though I doubt it. Anyway, I was well able to swim back to the jetty and with a degree of self-assurance which now seems hardly justified, I told the other lads not to worry.

I would go up to the Café at the top of the jetty and have a couple of drinks while the obliging proprietor and his staff dried my clothes.

Not to worry, I said with airy confidence, I would be back on board just an hour or so late, which only meant losing a day's pay and a day's leave. It was a matter of no great consequence.

So off up the jetty I went and into the Café. Sure enough, the good people therein were only too pleased to help. My clothes were promptly removed, washed and hung up to dry while I, gracefully attired in a Japanese robe not unlike the one in which I had enjoyed the Geishas ministrations, reclined gracefully with my drink.

Meanwhile, back at the jetty, things were not going quite according to plan. The ship's boat came in with a particularly keen midshipman in command.

He asked where I was. My mates (?) all said, with one voice, that I was up at the Café at the top of the jetty.'

'We can't let him be adrift' said the midshipman, concerned as he was for my welfare. 'Go up and fetch him'.

Not a word from the lads; up they came at the double and my life of Japanese luxury ended as abruptly as it had begun.

I sat there, master of all I surveyed, attired only in my kimono-like robe, a pair of sandals and a red straw hat. The sailors grabbed me unceremoniously and began to manhandle me down to the jetty.

I protested violently but it was no good. If the midshipman was surprised to see them returning from their mission with such a colourful figure in robe and straw hat, he didn't exactly show it. Before I fully realised what had happened I was in the boat, we had cast off and were on our way back to the ship.

On our arrival alongside my mates all went aboard, climbing the gangway, saluting the quarterdeck and getting ticked off for coming off shore late. Then it was my turn.

In a situation like that there is nothing to do but brave it out. I stepped boldly up the gangway, appeared somewhat incongruously on deck and, with my sandals, kimono and straw hat adding a splash of oriental glamour to the scene, snapped up a smart naval salute in the general direction of the quarter deck.

The 'quarter deck' was not exactly amused; at least, not in front of the men, that is! I was put into the Captain's report for being a disgrace to the King's uniform, coming on board improperly dressed and several other crimes.

It all added up to seven day's pay and leave lost – which, looking back, wasn't so bad, I suppose. After all, it is not every sailor who can say he once saluted his Captain wearing a straw hat and a kimono!

# 15 · The China Station

From Nagasaki we went back to China, which was – for us during our time ashore in what we called the French city – a city of cabarets and dance halls. There must have been twenty or more in that area and they were run after the American style. You paid ten cents for a dance and maybe dancing was not the only service offered for the right price.

I also had a spell of shore patrol, working with the English police and studying their different routines.

But it was the Chinese authorities, with their ideas of law and punishment, who gave me my most memorable experience of this period in my service. The Chinese criminal classes must either have been reckless or desperate men for they had only to steal something to run the risk of being very promptly beheaded.

I saw several executions. The prisoners would be paraded through the streets, accompanied by the executioners with their long axe-like knives. When the prisoners reached the square where they were to be executed their wrists were tied to their ankles and, in this kneeling position, they had no choice but to put their heads forward. Efficiently, the executioners went down the line, lopping off the heads.

Theft seemed to be considered the most serious crime in China. A shopkeeper who had accused a man of stealing from him could have the thief's head after execution. This he would hang in a basket at the front of his shop, rather as an English farmer might hang dead crows over his fields, as a deterrent to others who might be minded to make off with his property.

The fact that the executions continued might well suggest that the deterrent was not always effective or that the desperation induced by poverty was extreme.

After our spell in Shanghai we started our voyage up the great Yangtse river, stopping first at Nanking to give a few hours leave.

The thing we found of interest ashore here was a temple, built as a memorial to some past Chinese leader. It was at the top of a hill and reached by a thousand steps.

There were Chinese who, for a fee, would carry visitors up these hundreds of steps, but we weren't British sailors for nothing. We decided to hoof it up there under our own steam and we made it, just. But boy, were we tired! We had to rest awhile before entering the temple.

But it was worth it. The temple was full of the most beautiful oriental carving and ornamentation I had ever seen.

Our job, however, was not to stand around admiring temples. Our ship was soon continuing up river; way up river and ever deeper into the heart of China.

We were heading for Hankow, quite a large city and almost a thousand miles up the great Yangtse river from the sea.

Our duties as guard ship at Hankow were many and varied. One was to send patrols in all passenger boats plying between Hankow and the villages even further up river. Another was to put guards on all the merchantmen that came up.

The reason for both these duties was the ever present risk of looting.

We had very good evidence of this when we received a distress call from a ship somewhere between Hankow and Nanking. We upped anchor and steamed down river as fast as we could but we were too late.

The ship had run aground and her crew had been massacred. Every movable thing had been taken out of the ship, all in a matter of twelve to fifteen hours.

Even the steam pipes, copper pipes and all the engine fittings – everything, in fact, that could be unbolted and moved – had gone. From a nine thousand ton merchant vessel she had been reduced, in that short space of time, to just an old useless hulk.

It would have taken a British dockyard months to pull apart the inside of a ship that size, but the Chinese had done it in hours.

There must have been an army of them, running into hundreds, and how they managed to lift some of the heavy gear and machinery is a mystery I shall never solve now. But they did it and left just a bare hulk.

Back in Hankow, I had a dollop of good luck. It came about, unusually for me, through being in the right place at the right time, rather than following my more usual habit of being in the right place to get into trouble!

To explain: One of the most picturesque sights in Hankow was afforded us by the floating villages that came down river. They were formed by the woodsmen who cut down the trees alongside the upper reaches of the Yangtse and built them into a gigantic raft.

As a means of getting the wood down river the idea was unrivalled, for the trees were both cargo and vessel, and on to such a raft the woodsmen moved his house, his water buffalo, pigs, chickens and family, until there was a whole village assembled on the raft.

Then they would cast off and come down river with the tide, past Hankow to Nanking where they broke up the raft and sold the timber. I should think, for the woodsmen, the journey home was rather more laborious than the voyage down river.

One day I was on deck taking a photograph of one of these immense rafts when I suddenly spotted an aeroplane that seemed to be in distress.

Now, at this point, I should remind you that this was the 1920s and an aeroplane in good order was by no means a commonplace sight, let alone one which appeared to be in difficulty.

I watched as it tried to land but it didn't quite make it. As the aeroplane crashed I clicked the shutter; and that is how I recorded an embarrassing moment in the life of that great aviator, Colonel Lindbergh, the man who had crossed the Atlantic single handed and had also been in the news over the kidnapping of his son.

Why the great man came to be piloting an aircraft in distress over Hankow, I don't know, but in my camera was the only photograph taken of the crash.

Well, when you've got something good, you don't keep it to yourself, so I sold the picture to the Shanghai News for five hundred dollars. For a time, the money was held by the ship's Captain because nobody was quite sure whether or not I had broken Navy regulations. But Stan's luck held and I eventually got the money.

One day, there was a big celebration on shore so some friends and I, curious as ever, got leave and attended. You'll never guess what all the fuss was about; a public execution! As if I hadn't already seen enough of that sort of thing in Shanghai.

There was the same old parade through the streets, the prisoners accompanied by the men with the long knives. Up they went to the top of a hill, their hands were tied to their ankles and the heads rolled. Life was cheap.

I think there must have been about twenty executed that day, but they could almost reckon themselves the lucky ones, for, at the top of the hill, was a torture field where prisoners were subjected to the most unimaginable horrors.

Some were simply in ordinary stocks, like the traditional English ones and people were throwing all manner of offal and rubbish at them.

Others were chained to a stake, each with a large wooden collar round his neck so he couldn't feed himself. These poor wretches depended for life on the scraps people threw at them and, how long they were kept there, I do not know. Still others were strapped down over bamboo shoots which gradually grew right through their bodies. Yet more were buried up to their necks in anthills so the ants gradually devoured them.

It was a sickening sight for our western eyes, though almost a kind of entertainment for the locals and we did not linger long enough to find out what terrible crimes these unfortunate people had committed to warrant such an agonising end.

I did a couple of turns as guard on a merchantman and on ferry boats and then I was lent to HMS *Glowworm*. She was one of the famous flat-bottomed Yangtse River gunboats of the Navy at that time, boats that have their own very special place in the history of the Royal Navy and that bred a special kind of sailors bonded together by a special kind of comradeship.

They – and I, while I was with them – saw China as she really was as we patrolled the upper reaches of the great Yangtse River.

We saw women with feet bound from birth and, consequently, so small they could have no hope of running. Very often we saw women come down to the water's edge, give birth and then go back to their work in the paddy fields.

Life was hard as well as cheap and it all seemed to centre on the great river along which we, in our flat-bottomed gunboat, patrolled.

We went up river until we reached rapids which were too fierce for the old *Glowworm* to get through unaided. So hundreds of Chinese were recruited, great teams of them on either side of the river with huge ropes snaking back to our fo'c'stle.

With the engines going full ahead and the Chinese pulling, we got through the rapids and reached the calmer water above.

Life on board was very similar to that in a destroyer, happy-go-lucky and with not too much discipline. We all had our jobs to do and we did them without supervision.

At night we would show only the barest glimmer of light on the upper deck, *Glowworm* both by name and appearance, for it would attract thousands of insects; rice flies there were and great flying crabs, or 'doodlebugs' as we called them. Maybe that was the origin of the name for this was long before Hitler's doodlebugs came on the scene.

If these Chinese doodlebugs hit you the collision would break the skin and give you a nasty cut. We swept them up in heaps under the small lamps we carried on the upper deck.

We went ashore for exercises though there was great fun in it. There was very little to do, and no beer to drink, apart from our daily ration of one bottle, and even that was onion beer and not worth drinking.

On shore one day Stan and his mates bought a baby donkey. Our idea was to take the animal on board and keep it as a mascot; but, of course, this was against the rules.

You will have gathered by now that Stan was not a person necessarily to be dissuaded from doing something he really wanted to do, just because it was against the rules. Rules, even in the Navy, were always there to be bent.

So, we smuggled the donkey on board and took it down to the store room.

This involved getting the animal through a circular hatch – rather like those in submarines – and into the room where all the ship's stores were kept and in which we built a stall with cotton waste bales to conceal the donkey from sight.

Our donkey was not discovered, not even during Captain's rounds when the Commanding Officer would go down to check the stores.

Going back through the rapids – with our donkey mascot hidden safely below – we must have done about 25 knots with the roaring bubbling water carrying us through to the Yangtse. And so, back to Hankow where I had to rejoin my ship.

But that, for me, was certainly not the last I heard of the old *Glowworm* and her donkey. The 'mascot' grew and grew until it was much too big to get through the store-room hatch and until, one day, the inevitable happened and the animal was discovered.

They had to take a complete plate out of the side of the ship to get the donkey out and the chaps involved in that escapade all got stiff punishments.

But Stan was long gone and, anyway, back in Hankow I had other things on my mind.

Our duties at Hankow were pretty arduous. Junks were continually fouling the ship and we also had to keep a sharp look-out for the floating villages which came down on the tide with no means of control other than a couple of sweeps stuck out of the back of the raft.

These were useless in a seven to eight knot tide and the rafts would crash into our ship and run down her side.

There was very little doing on shore; no cabarets or entertainments of any kind except one or two bars that sold onion beer. But there was a good canteen ashore where we could get McEwans' nips and English beer. Needless to say, we were frequently in the canteen.

After our time expired as guard ship at Hankow we sailed back down the river past Nanking and on to the open sea. In Shanghai, where our ship went alongside Harland and Wolfe's wharf for minor repairs, we were back to a more lively run ashore.

We duly gave the cabarets and bars a good deal of our custom and enjoyed the meals served in the American Club.

After repairs had been completed we went back to Whe Hi Whe, to another small town where there was a railway. Leave was given to anyone who wished to visit Peking.

With three other chaps I went to the Chinese capital and we had a wonderful time, staying in quite a good hotel and visiting some of Peking's temples.

In those days the great Chinese temples were the pride of Peking. Mao was still way into the future and Buddha reigned supreme.

There was the Temple of Sorrow, the Temple of Joy, the beautiful Temple of Heaven; I forget many of the names. They were set in the most beautiful grounds and the people would leave food and money in front of the Buddha for the priests to collect later.

The Chinese people were extremely polite. They even took their glasses off when they spoke to you to avoid seeing you as a false image.

We engaged three rickshaw boys who knew all the city's 'hot spots' and the cold ones and they took us everywhere. But, as life in the Navy constantly proves, you can't stay in one place for long, and it was soon time for us to rejoin the *Cumberland*.

We caught the train; but what a train! Although we had first class tickets the carriage we occupied was more like a cattle truck.

You could not see out of the windows for the bodies of the third class passengers outside, clinging on to any hand or foot-hold they could find.

And so we travelled back to our ship, submerged under a moving heap of human bodies.

The ship sailed back to Whe Hi Whe for gunnery and torpedo trials in the bay and for some pretty unexpected 'acts of God'.

# 16 · The 'Poseidon' Incident

Four years I spent in HMS *Cumberland* on the China Station – between December, 1929 and February 1933 – and they were four of the most eventful years of my life in the Royal Navy.

We used to go to Whe Hi Whe for recreation and for gunnery and torpedo exercises and we would normally stay there about a month at a time. There was quite a nice harbour and we spent much of our time in sailing. I won several bottles of beer for winning races in the cutters against the Commander.

There was a canteen on shore about a mile away from the landing jetty. Beer was reasonably priced and our usual meal was a Whe Hi Whe Runner. This consisted of a whole chicken with chips and it cost the magnificent sum of 1s 6d (7½p).

The table was always piled high with peanuts which were offered free by the management on the theory that they made customers thirsty and therefore they drank more beer.

In the village there were no real shops; just shacks with open frontages where the wares could be displayed.

You could get pretty well anything done ashore that you wanted. The sailors used to have their collars turned inside out and retaped. Even better, if you had a serge suit that was past its best you could get it turned inside out and it would look almost new.

Any job that needed doing you could get done ashore, no matter how large or small. They would do your laundry, mend your shoes and generally see after your welfare, and all manner of food could be bought to be taken back on board.

Although the routine of the China Station stays in my mind, it was interrupted by all sorts of unexpected hazards; accidents, acts of violence and excesses of the Far Eastern climate.

The accident which remains among my most vivid, if not exactly my most pleasant, memories might best be described as the Poseidon Incident.

From where I was, the sequence of events unfolded as follows . . .

74

HMS *Cumberland* lay in Whe Hi Whe harbour. Nothing seemed at all out of the ordinary that morning when special sea duty men were piped to their stations, the ship weighed anchor and got under way at 0800 hours heading out of harbour towards the China Sea.

Just another torpedo or gunnery exercise; that's what we thought.

Once outside the harbour we went to general quarters, guns were tested, circuits were tested and all the normal procedures were followed of a warship on exercises or getting herself in a state of readiness for what action might present itself.

Then we went to cruising stations and from there, at 8.30, we went to breakfast.

After that we dropped a target and circled it, firing electro tubes ammunition. This consists of a tube fitted inside the large guns and firing only small rounds of ammunition.

While we were going through this exercise we passed fairly close to a merchant ship which signalled that she was thought to have struck a submerged vessel – probably a submarine – and that oil had appeared on the surface along with a small amount of wreckage.

We proceeded to the position given by the merchant ship but could see nothing.

The Captain piped for volunteer boat crews – preferably to man pulling boats – and the message had no sooner been piped than all the boats were fully manned.

I took the second cutter and fourteen good sailors volunteered to come in with me. We were lowered and a grapnel was placed in the boat. We were told to grapple along a line parallel to the ship.

There was about an eight knot current running, which made it hard work pulling up against the current. So we worked with the current, trailing the grapnel astern.

We did this all morning and at about 12.30 the corned beef sandwiches and hot tea and cocoa sent out from the ship were more than welcome.

Suddenly, about an hour later, our grapnel caught up with something on the bottom. We tried to shift the grapnel. We pulled on it, but we couldn't move it at all, so I signalled back to the ship.

There was great excitement in the ship when they knew we had caught something up in our grapnel. Marker buoys were sent out and they had to be placed well above where I was to allow for the tides.

By this time, several ships had arrived on the scene and were standing by. One of them was an American vessel which carried deep sea divers who were going down to try to locate what was underneath us.

Their task, too, was not made any easier by the strong current.

We were just idly pulling the boat to keep stationary against the current and to keep in position near the flags marking the spot where the submarine was thought to be.

Around mid-afternoon there was suddenly a tremendous upheaval in the water and up bobbed seven human beings.

Half my crew were over the side in a flash, swimming out to bring the survivors back to the boat.

When we got them into the boat we found that their faces and necks were so black and swollen that it was impossible to get the Davis escape gear from them without cutting it away. Fortunately, I had a nice sharp knife handy and I did just that.

We got them on board and managed to pump some air into them and then started to take them back to our ship. About half way there the motor boat came and collected them and took them the rest of the way to HMS *Cumberland*.

Soon after we had got back to our station four more submariners suddenly bobbed up to the surface. They were all in a bad state, but we managed to get them on board, cut off their gear and revive them.

One of the survivors was a Chinese cook and he seemed to be in the worst shape of all. He was almost gone.

Giving him artificial respiration, we pumped and pumped away at him and very slowly he passed on.

The motor boat came alongside and took us in tow and thus we headed back to the *Cumberland*. We didn't know whether there were any more survivors to come, but there were now plenty of boats and ships around to take care of them.

Later we were to learn something about the ordeal that the submariners had gone through on the sea bottom and how they owed their lives to the experience, presence of mind and bravery of their chief coxswain.

Apparently, the submarine had been hit just abaft the conning tower and the whole after part of the boat – complete with crew members inside – had been lost.

In the fore part there were eleven men, including the Chinese cook and the chief coxswain, a chap by the name of Chief Petty Officer Willis. This man undoubtedly saved the lives of the ten others.

First, he led them in prayer, and they sang a hymn. Then they rigged up jackstays along the bulkhead so that they could stand on them with their mouths close against the roof of the submarine.

Meanwhile, CPO Willis encouraged them all and got them into their Davis escape apparatus which, in those days, only really consisted of a mask.

They all stood on the jackstays around the hatch and Mr Willis gradually flooded the compartment by opening the valves until the pressure in the submarine was more than the pressure of the water above the hatch.

It was when the hatch sprang open that the eleven men escaped to live to tell us their story and to tell us that the name of their submarine was HMS *Poseidon*.

Some weeks after the event we had to attend a Court of Inquiry in Hong Kong and I got hauled over the coals by a Commander who said I had no business cutting the Davis gear away. I should have pulled it clear or unbuttoned it, he declared.

I am afraid I spoke out of turn, telling him that it had been a choice between saving the Davis escape gear or the lives of the men inside it. He didn't go much on being told off in these terms and I was instructed to pipe down forthwith.

For CPO Willis there was a hero's welcome when he got back to England. In fact, the *Daily Mirror* started a fund and a bungalow was built for the coxswain in gratitude for his act of bravery.

I learned afterwards that my grapnel had caught in the brass handrail that goes around the conning tower because, later, in a ship which was holding the grapnel, somebody had taken a turn round a cleat and the grapnel had suddenly pulled the brass handrail off the submarine.

We had to assume that the men we had seen come to the surface were the only survivors of the *Poseidon*. Down on the bottom the American divers had tapped all around the hull but had received no answering sounds from inside.

# 17 · Acts of God

We didn't know it at the time, but a newcomer was about to enter our lives; a boy we called Chick, a real life orphan of the storm.

In Whe Hi Whe boys came on board voluntarily to look after each mess. They would prepare the meals, wash up, go ashore to buy the provisions and they would do all this just for what was left in the dishes after a meal.

The 'gash' was all the payment they asked.

To supplement this meagre reward we would club together to give them a few dollars at the end of a trip.

You see, we couldn't take North Country boys with us down to Hong Kong or Shanghai because the Southern boys would only fight with them for the privilege of working for us and the result would have been that we would have got no food!

We did a cruise around the Yellow Sea, visiting various volcanic islands and also the island of Formosa, now Taiwan.

We just had time for a run ashore there before the ship received an urgent call to go back to the Yangtse. The great river was in flood and what grim tasks awaited us.

The river had burst its banks and there was water on both sides as far as the eye could see. Small communities had been engulfed, the water lapping around the roofs of the houses and homeless villagers were desperately trying to salvage some of their belongings, using rafts and gaining access to their dwellings by making holes in the roofs.

There were bodies floating down the river, so many of them you could not begin to describe the scene. Buffalo, cattle, pigs, people. I have never seen so many bodies in all my life, not all at once, anyway.

We went back up to Hankow and started rescue operations, using every available ship's boat and taking them as far inland as possible.

They sailed over telegraph poles, football fields, villages and all devastated relics of human occupation.

After a spell in the boats a man was allowed ashore to visit the canteen. The motor boats steamed up the main street to the six or seven canteen steps which had all but saved it from the floods, there being only about a foot of water inside.

But what did a foot of water matter when, after such harrowing work, we were intent only on getting a couple of bottles of beer inside us.

The rescue operations continued for some time. I remember pulling a man out of the Yangtse only to see him jump straight back in again. Buddha had declared that he was to die in the Yangtse and who was I to stand in the way of fate?

On another occasion a raft came down river with a small boy entwined in the lashings. We got him on board and he told us, through an interpreter, that his mother and father had been washed away and he was the only member of his family left.

We adopted him, christened him Chick and, as Captain's cox'n by this time, I had quite a lot to do with kitting out and training of our new Chinese cabin boy or number three hand.

We dressed him appropriately for his new role in life and he learned, quite quickly, to speak English. He would prepare the vegetables and make himself useful in many other ways.

He turned out to be a very good cabin boy and was eventually taken on officially by the Royal Navy. After we had paid off at the end of that eventful Commission the next lot of Cumberlands 'inherited' Chick and he remained with the ship as one of the Captain's valets.

After Hankow we went back right down to Hong Kong where leave was given and the decks were daily filled by the local trades people.

The 'sew-sew' girls, the cobblers and the tradesmen selling many and varied commodities, brought the seething world of Hong Kong commerce right on board our ship. The 'sew-sew' girls were particularly helpful, turning our worn-out collars and maybe making an old suit look as good as new.

The cobblers mended our shoes and the laundry girls took away the dirty linen, not worrying if we were called away on a sudden mission but assuming they would get their money when we returned.

We would go ashore up on the peak where there was a good restaurant and also across by ferry to Kowloon where we spent our time hunting for souvenirs and curios to take home to our families.

But before that could happen the unpredictable Asian climate, prone to extremes, was to take a hand in our fortunes again. We had seen the devastation and misery caused by China's great flood, now we were to experience, at first hand, the effects of a hurricane.

Immediately on receiving the warning, the ship was prepared as if for action.

Awnings were taken down and all stanchions and everything movable securely lashed down. When the hurricanes hit us we had two anchors down and steam up to go slow ahead to keep the anchors holding.

I have never seen wind and rain like it. It blew so that, if you forgot to hold on to something, you were swept along the deck.

It was terrible. An auxiliary oil tanker, lying just off the dockyard wall, was lifted bodily out of the water and deposited some fifty to sixty yards inshore. After the hurricane she had to be dismantled and reassembled in dry dock before she could be refloated.

The storm did enormous damage. Junks and sampans, which crowded the harbour, had disappeared as if by magic. They had heard the forecast and scurried away to shelter. The harbour seemed totally deserted.

Tremendous damage was also done on shore and there was a great clearing up operation to be done when the hurricane had gone.

Our Captain, Sir Eric Eggerson, was a strict man for discipline and procedure, and as Captain's cox'n, I had quite a busy time. The Captain's gig had never before been used for ceremonial occasions so I had to get the boat painted inside and out and we had to use sharkskin over the thwarts and oars.

Mentioning the oars of the Captain's gig, it now seems proper to point out that these impressive implements were no less than seventeen feet long. Since rowing a ceremonial gig is very different from rowing an ordinary boat, I had to train the crew in the procedure.

We also had to make all the 'tiddly gear' that goes with a ceremonial boat. The yoke lines we made of white cord with Turk's heads, bound them with canvas and drill and plaited them with duck and bluejean strips. We made large tassels for the ends of the yokes, using Turk's heads, pineapple knots and all the pretty things which sailors can devise with ropes.

We also had to make cushions for the sternsheets and mats where the Captain would step into the boat from the ship's gangway.

The whole job took quite a long time, but our efforts paid off, and the result was well worth looking at. We went on several ceremonial trips taking the Captain from one ship to another and the boat caused quite a stir.

The Captain also had a full Chinese staff which came under my watchful eye. There was a carpenter who would polish the tables and maintain all the woodwork, doing minor repairs and making artistic gangways and handrails to the upper decks.

There was also a Chinese wine steward, two cooks and two 'makey learn' boys, one of whom was Chick.

The Captain certainly lived the life of an aristocrat on board his command for, in addition to the aforementioned staff, two Chinese valets also tended to his every need.

For me, however, the management of this inscrutable crew posed considerable problems of diplomacy. Their greatest fear was to lose 'face' and this was inevitable if they were ever openly accused of doing wrong.

If one of them was caught stealing it was necessary to go first to his superior and tell him that something was missing and gradually the message would be passed on. It was essential that a thief must never be confronted with his crime face to face.

By this time we Cumberlands had completed our two and a half years on the China Station so we began our journey home. We did exercises with the RAF in the Malay Straits and then spent a couple of days in Singapore, going ashore, buying souvenirs and exploring the town. After a similar call at Colombo we went on to Aden, through the Red Sea, Suez Canal and Mediterranean on our way back home, to arrive, early one morning, off Sheerness in the Medway.

You could be forgiven for thinking that, back in home waters and with the ship on the point of paying off, this long and adventurous Commission would have no more experiences and escapades to offer us. You would be wrong, for we were not 'home and dry' just yet. At Sheerness we still had to contend with the River Patrol.

Not to put too fine a point on it, they were a nasty lot. The only people on board during the silent hours of the night were the quartermaster, officer of the watch and a sentry on the fo'c'stle.

The quartermaster had to challenge all boats that were passing or coming alongside. The officer of the watch invariably stayed down in his cabin until he was required.

The habit of the river patrol was to drift down river with the tide, with their engine turned off. They would wait until the quartermaster had gone into the galley to make himself a cup of cocoa, then they would sneak on board and take a lifebuoy or something that was handy near the gangway.

Away they would go, only to come back in the morning to present their 'loot' to the Captain and tell him that there had been no-one on duty, guarding the ship. This invariably meant that the quartermaster would be punished for leaving his post and perhaps the sentry would get it in the neck, as well.

The river patrol tried this a couple of times until we got fed up with it and decided to take counter measures. We decided to form a reception committee.

We lay patiently in wait one night, armed with potatoes, eggs and any other produce we could lay our hands on. Eventually, our patience was rewarded. The black shape of a silent boat, drifting along on the tide, emerged from the night.

Suddenly, all hell broke loose. We pelted them with our 'ammo', scoring several direct hits and they soon buzzed off. oddly enough, they never bothered us again, not until after we went up to Chatham, that is.

It was there that the *Cumberland* was due to go into dock. When we moored in the basin to pay off we had come to the end of a Commission which I don't think anybody on board could ever forget. The Royal Navy, between the wars, was a benign policeman with a beat covering all the world's seas, but of all the areas in which it served none could have been more strange, more fascinating or more brutal, whether in the behaviour of its people, its climate or its insects, than the China Station.

I said goodbye to Chick and promised, like we all do, to give him my address so that he could write to me in the future. Chick, that small piece of human flotsam from the floods who became a sailor in His Majesty's Royal Navy, was just one small person who had taken a gigantic leap to cross the gap between the West and the mystic East. Many more have followed him since.

# 18 · 'What shall we do with . . .'

A sailor's adventures are not necessarily over once he has climbed off his ship in his home port and set off for a spot of leave; especially if you are an East Anglian country boy and you happen, by chance, to meet a shipmate who comes from the same neck of woods as you do.

Andrew Doddington and I lived only two or three miles apart, back home in the Waveney Valley, but we didn't know it. All that time we had been serving on the same ships. We'd been to the Mediterranean together, but although we knew each other vaguely, we didn't meet properly until we got back to Chatham and happened to choose the same pub for a drink.

But when we did eventually get together, I can tell you we certainly made up for lost time. It happened like this . . .

We had arrived at Chatham and gone through the usual preliminaries with the Customs people and we were all ready to proceed on leave.

I had several things to take home, including a Japanese teaset which was all packed up beautifully in a nice box. I was very pleased with this particular souvenir.

There was some delay on board so we missed the ten o-clock train from Chatham to London. That didn't worry us too much and I decided to while away the time by going to the nearest pub and getting back my taste for English beer.

The first priority was to get a drink, the second to find a seat, so it wasn't until I was sitting there with a pint in my fist that I could look around at those other members of the ship's company who were in the bar.

The face of one of them was vaguely familiar, although I hadn't known him a lot in the ship or on the Commission. It was Andrew Doddington and we got into conversation.

I asked him where he came from and he said 'Just outside Beccles'. 'What?' said I, and the look of surprise on my face must have told him something for he added; 'Well, from Sotterly, which is only a couple of miles outside Beccles.

I had hardly had time to respond; 'Cor, lovely . . .' or words to that effect, when the conversation, and the beer, began to flow ever more easily.

Naturally, we decided to travel home together, but it was to be an eventful journey.

Having got as far as London, we missed the 3.10 pm train, which was the one we had aimed for, so we decided to go and have a drink at 'Dirty Dick's'.

Not only did we have a few drinks, but we also each bought a presentation pack containing half-bottles of rum, whisky and gin. The idea was that these would make nice little presents for the folks back home.

Of course, I was still lugging my Japanese tea-set about, and very proudly too, although it was beginning to get a bit in the way.

Well, we eventually caught a train somewhere about five o-clock and it was a very boring journey. It was a slow train which stopped at practically every station so, to relieve the tedium, we started on our presentation packs of booze.

There was very little to see out of the window as night closed in and, what was more natural, but to refresh ourselves and keep on doing so.

Truth to tell, there wasn't an awful lot of our presentation packs left by the time the guard put us off the train at Beccles. There, on the platform, ready to greet two drunken sailors who didn't really know what day of the week it was, or where they were, was my father.

Dad was quite concerned – which, looking back, I suppose was fairly understandable – about the Japanese tea-set. In fact, even in my far gone state I got the distinct impression that Dad wanted to take charge of it. But no, I was determined to prove I was fit enough to carry it on my shoulder.

And I did, without mishap!

So he fell in behind us and we rolled happily up Station Road towards the centre of the town.

We were making for the CROSS KEYS pub (which has long since closed), partly because we were still thirsty and partly because Andrew kept his bike there. For him, the last part of a journey home from the China Station, was a three mile bike ride in the dark along the country roads to Sotterley.

On the way to the CROSS KEYS we stopped at Barber's, the tobacconist shop in Smallgate and Andrew bought a pound of shag which they did up in a brown paper parcel. This he stuffed into his jersey.

While we were 'topping up' our drink level in the CROSS KEYS somebody saw this bit of brown paper sticking out of Andrew's jersey and pulled it out. Tobacco fell out everywhere and went all over Andrew's chest and belly.

That was all right by Andrew. Both of us were far too well away to worry about a small thing like that.

So we put Andrew on his bike, pointed him in the right direction, said our goodbyes, gave him a shove and off he went.

Now, Andrew was known to his friends as 'Nutty' and never did he earn his nickname more than during that eventful bike ride from Beccles to Sotterley.

I got to hear all about it the following day when I went to see his mother.

Apparently Andrew got almost to Sotterley, nearly into the village, when he experienced the call of nature which told him it was time to get rid of some of that beer.

So, Andrew and bike rolled up and leaned against a five-barred gate. The road was lonely, everywhere was quiet and Nutty stayed awake just about long enough to breathe a sigh of relief. Then, still draped over the gate, he fell deeply asleep.

Well, it so happens that it was the habit of the Vicar's wife to ride her tricycle along that particular stretch of road and she came pedalling along through the village and past Andrew on her way to the vicarage.

Dimly, in the half-light, she spotted a figure – much like a scarecrow – propped up on a five-barred gate. It says much for Nutty that she recognised him at once and called 'Hello Andrew'. No answer.

So she called again and again there was no answer. He just lay on the gate, quite oblivious to all that was going on around him.

So the vicar's wife got off her three-wheeler and went over to give Andrew a shake, whereupon he promptly collapsed in a heap on the ground.

The good lady was in a terrible panic. She got back on her trike and rode furiously back to the village to get help. As a result, two men with a farm hurdle came to collect the sailor who had come home from the sea.

Once home, his mother undressed him, shook his clothes out and wiped his face. The tobacco had made its mark and Andrew had come out in a terrible rash all over his chest and stomach.

So the doctor was called and the village was not likely to forget in a hurry old Nutty's return from the China Station.

We had some great high jinks, Andrew and I, around the Beccles area.

At that particular time, our reward after two and a half years on the China Station was twenty eight days' leave. Around Beccles, in a region where many earned their living on the farms and others with the fishing – and some were 'half and halfers' – nobody was much interested in the stories told by a sailor home from the other side of the world.

Anyway, I had little time to look back on my adventures, for life was there to be lived at a hectic pace, even when you were on leave.

Somehow I got bitten by the motorbike bug and bought myself a 1910 strap driven Douglas on which I was soon zipping about the countryside. It was necessary to put vinegar on the driving wheel of the strap to ensure a good grip.

I used to ride out to Sotterley and pick up Andrew and away we went all around the countryside, calling at the pubs and generally enjoying ourselves.

On one occasion we went to Beccles livestock market and we were having a good old time, bidding against the farmers to knock up the prices. They realised it and we got caught; half a dozen piglets were knocked down to us.

There was nothing we could do except pay up and somehow get the pigs back to Sotterley where Andrew's father looked after them.

Sometime later, when we got back from a Commission in HMS *MacKay*, Andrew's dad gave us a fiver each from the money he had made by the sale of those pigs.

I used to stay at Andrew's house and one day when we had had quite a session – the beer, I think, was a little cloudy – I blotted my copybook with a vengeance.

I blush even now when I remember how that cloudy beer went straight through me and took me by surprise. I was too late when I got to the toilet so all I could do was to take my naval knickers off and clean myself up.

Greatly embarrassed, I just didn't know what to do with my pants. Houses at Sotterley, in those days, didn't boast anything more than a privy with a bucket which was emptied every day on the garden.

I got a spade, dug a hole and dropped these knickers of mine into it, filled it in and that was that. At least, that was what I thought, but how wrong I was!

Some time later, when I was back home after serving in the *MacKay*, I went to see Andrew's mum again and she greeted me with the news 'I've got something of yours, Stan, it's up in the drawer in Andrew's bedroom'.

I said 'Oh yes, what's that?'

'A pair of knickers,' she said.

'Where the devil did you get those from?' I asked.

'Well, the dog was shaking them up and down the garden!' she replied.

Motor bikes – then as now – were regarded as something of an aid to romance and my old Douglas was no exception. This machine tempted a young lady called Olive to come out with me for a couple of 'spins'.

With a bike like that a fellow could take a girl to the pictures at Yarmouth and away we went with Olive riding pillion.

Having parked the bike at a garage in Regent Road, we settled down to enjoy the film. At the interval I decided to go down and buy a box of chocolates, a very romantic thought, of course. But you know how plans can go wrong and a chap can get sidetracked.

On the way down to get the chocolates I decided to nip into the bar for a quick one. Who should I see in there but three old chums from my schooldays at Yarmouth.

Well, you know how it is. We got talking, memories flowed as the beer flowed and we lost all count of time and place.

It seemed like a good idea when somebody suggested we should carry on this happy meeting at the Queen's Hotel and so we did – until closing time.

By the time we emerged from the Queen's Hotel we were, I admit, tending to look upon the world through rose hued spectacles and with a song in our hearts and on our lips.

Life was good, friends were firm and – well, to tell the truth, this is one small part of my story I don't remember too well.

Somebody got my Douglas, kicked it into life for me, pointed me in the right direction and my safe arrival home is a mystery never to be unravelled. Thank heavens they hadn't invented the breathilyser.

Mother had laid the table for me and there was a complete leg of pork, some pickled cabbage in a small dish and also a large jar alongside it. It was a feast fit for a king and, so I believe, I feasted right royally before getting undressed and going to bed.

My recollections of the night were decidedly hazy when Mother brought me up a cup of tea the following morning. 'I'm glad you had a good supper last night' she said with a kind of glint in her eye that I somehow didn't remember seeing before.

'Oh, I don't think I did,' said I, wondering what was coming next. 'I didn't really feel very hungry.'

'Well, put your trousers on and come down and have a look at what you ate,' invited Mother.

Down I went, to find that I had eaten all the 'crackling' from the leg of pork and then made V signs in what was left of it with the carving knife.

I had ignored the pickled cabbage in the dish but had taken it from the large jar, leaving vivid red cobwebs of pickled cabbage vinegar across the white tablecloth.

I was ashamed, but my shame was nothing compared with the guilt brought on by my mother's next question. 'However did you get on with that girl, Olive?' she asked, all innocently.

Olive? Oh, THAT Olive! Oh no, I'd left the poor girl in the cinema, waiting for a box of chocolates that had never arrived.

I washed and dressed, got on my bike and belted off to Yarmouth, though what, or who, I expected to find, I don't know. I went to the police who said yes, she had been there and they had taken her home. You see, she had no money on her, poor girl.

Feeling somewhat on the small side, I put some money into the orphan's box and, well, that was, sort of . . . that.

I never saw poor Olive again and never had a chance to apologise.

# 19 · Back with the Big Shots

When my leave was finished I went back to Chatham Barracks and to the gunnery school were I resumed my duties as gunnery instructor.

I took several classes through for seaman gunner and learned just how frustrating this work could be.

You could have a perfect class, excelling in every aspect of the job and passing out with merit. Then you might go to the office and learn that perhaps only five were to be passed for Seaman Gunner.

It meant not only disappointment for the rest of the class after eight weeks of hard slog, but also bitter frustration for their instructor.

One of the courses required the candidates to operate the night shooting battery. There they worked in complete darkness with a gun mounted on a platform driven by a motor to reproduce the motion of a ship.

Pitch, roll and yaw, it was enough to make a young man seasick.

The gun also produced a concussion resembling the recoil when the trigger was pulled. But on the gun controls in the night battery trainer was fitted nothing more lethal than an air rifle which fired a pellet at the target.

The target could also be kept moving, to right or left, by use of a motor and it was essential for the gunners to keep trained on the model of an enemy ship which represented their target.

I became well versed in the 'patter' it was necessary to give all classes in the night shooting battery. But there were some variations in the 'script' on the occasion when I had a class of Wrens who, being broad minded as all Wrens are, didn't seem to mind.

I don't know why the Wrens went through the night shooting battery; just for the sake of interest, I suppose.

To my shame, I do recall telling them in the darkness that if they found a thumb placed in their hand with no thumbnail on it, to drop it as it was no use to them!

Such were the ways of a sailor man. I don't suppose poor old Olive ever knew how lucky she was that night I disappeared at the cinema in Yarmouth!

But, back to the big shots of Chatham. When you started out with a new class there is no doubt you bullied them. You told them who their parents were – assuming you considered they had any – and how useless they were.

But, as they improved, confidence was gradually built up in the class, you in them and they in you. They came to realise that you were doing the best you could for them and from that point on their aim was to do their best for their instructor. It all became rather more like a happy family group than a class.

Once that relationship had been established the disappointment was so much greater when only half a successful class made it to Seaman Gunner. It usually took me a bit of solitude, and a couple of pints, to wash away the despondency.

But Stan never stayed despondent for long and soon I was looking forward eagerly to my next bit of sea service in HMS *York*. An 8-inch gun cruiser, she was due to go to North and South America, the 'jam station' as we used to call it.

These trips across the Atlantic tended not to involve much in the way of gunnery or torpedo exercises. They were regarded as being more like pleasure cruises.

The ship would do a cruise of three or four thousand miles extending right from the tip of South America to the icy wastes at the top end of Canada.

A sailor was also pretty well sure of a good run ashore, now and again, so can you wonder I was looking forward to the 'jam station'?.

# 20 · At Neptune's Court

We commissioned at Plymouth and, after the usual shakedown trials lasting about three weeks, we set sail for Rio de Janeiro. The first land we sighted was Cape St Vincent and soon after that we were due to 'cross the line'.

Crossing the line is a great ceremony in all ships – an excuse for a bit of fun, really – but there is nothing quite like the first time to imprint the occasion on a sailor's memory.

At ten that night 'King Neptune's Herald' came aboard and read the proclamation stating that King Neptune and his court would be in session at ten o-clock the following day. All 'Shellbacks' who had not been across the line before would be duly initiated as followers of King Neptune.

This was the signal for us to prepare for the following day's 'initiation ceremonies'.

All us old hands who had been across the line before got 'fell in' on the quarterdeck and were allotted our various jobs for the ceremonies. I was to be King Neptune's barber.

I mixed up a bucket of shaving lather and the carpenter made me a large wooden razor to enable me to 'operate' on the poor unfortunates who came before the King's court.

Preparations had been going on for several days to get the costumes ready. Mine consisted of a red and white gown and a tall top hat, also red and white. The idea was to suggest that I had a barber's pole on my head.

There were bears in shaggy costumes and policemen whose job would be to chase all the 'initiates' who were a bit shy about going through the ceremony.

Another central figure in this motley throng was Neptune's scribe who had a long flowing gown and a tall hat.

Just as the magic hour of ten arrived the following day, over the fo'c'stle came King Neptune with his scribe, his barber, his bears and policemen as part of quite a large retinue. With due dignity this regal figure from the depths of the ocean mounted his makeshift throne which was built up on a platform.

In front of the throne a chair had been set up on a swivel which could tilt it over backwards. Underneath, the bears waited around a large canvas bath, full of water.

The first 'customer' to go through the ritual was our Captain. He was first 'registered' by the scribe, then 'shaved' by the barber. Then the doctor gave him a couple of colourful pills and he was duly tipped over backwards into the canvas swimming pool.

The bears ducked him again and again until he bore more resemblance to a drowning, spluttering landlubber than a senior officer in His Majesty's Royal Navy.

He was just the first of many among our ship's company who went through the age old ritual that morning. It was quite a long sitting for King Neptune's court as some of the candidates for his favour were decidedly reluctant and had to be chased around the ship by his policemen.

Some even went so far as to climb the mast and rigging before they were caught and brought to Neptune's summary justice, being registered, shaved, given a pill and thrown into the pool.

Chaos reigned virtually all the morning, but at the end of it everyone in the ship was entitled to King Neptune's certificate.

Then suddenly it was all over. The 'King' and his court had disappeared back over the fo'c'stle and the routine of the ship took over again.

# 21 · Of Beef and Brothels

We steamed on and saw no more land, apart from the Cape Verde Islands, until we reached Rio where we went alongside the wall almost opposite the main street, a berth which gave us a good view of the town.

We had a good time on shore. Crowning a mountain at the back of the town was a statue of Christ with arms outstretched. It looked quite small in the distance, but when we went up there by the mountain railway, which ran up through the trees on the slopes, almost to the top, we could appreciate better the immense size of the statue.

We could also enjoy a magnificent view of the surrounding country, the city and the bays on either side.

In one of those bays was the Sugar Loaf Mountain which could be reached by an overhead railway some hundreds of feet in the air.

It was quite a thrill going across. As the cars swayed in the breeze it was almost possible to get sea-sick, or should I say air-sick. Anyway, it could hardly be rail-sick.

On top of the mountains were cabarets, dance halls and bars which, along with the swimming in the bays, made for one of the best runs ashore you could get.

In short, we had a real good time. The main street of Rio and its boulevards, if not exactly paved with gold, were laid out with gardens on one side and a mosaic pavement on the other.

The mosaic paving of the main street stretched way into the distance, flanked by a wide variety of shops and cabarets.

One of the great attractions of Rio was its huge brothel, three whole streets of it. By far the biggest I had ever seen, it was divided into separate quarters – the white, the Portuguese, Argentine and French quarters and all were quite strictly controlled.

Regular medical inspections were carried out. Even the customers were inspected. Any girl caught soliciting on the streets was sent to one of these brothels and remained there until she had no more urge for sex and then she was released.

We spent about three eventful weeks at Rio before sailing up the River Plate to the capital, Buenos Aires. The thing that most impressed me as we went up the river was the immense stack of horns, hooves and hides on the starboard bank.

Situated at Buenos Aires was the Fray Bentos beef factory. We had an opportunity to tour the factory and found it to be true that the bullocks were driven in at one end to come out in tins at the other.

It was the first time I had seen mass production and I was greatly impressed by it.

We spent about a fortnight in Buenos Aires, having our customary good time – I've never yet come across a port where Jack could not find something to amuse himself – and then we sailed back down the River Plate and around the infamous Horn to the Falkland Islands.

We went ashore to see the few homesteads of a tiny town where you could buy a whole sheep for a shilling and eat mutton for a week.

I have never seen mutton served up in so many different ways, but it made quite a difference to our mess bill. We were very grateful for it.

From the Falkland Islands we sailed back round the Horn to Jamaica where I visited the great natural lakes of pitch, a substance which, I learned, figured largely among Jamaica's exports.

Our patronage of the dance halls and other attractions contributed to another good time ashore, but I had another reason to remember Jamaica with affection.

One morning, as we were leaving the shore, the midshipman in charge of our boat told me that my Petty Officer rating had come through. I saw the Captain at about 11.00 am and duly assumed my new title.

My new role in life entailed moving out of the seamen's mess into that of the Petty Officers and it was not long before I noticed a few subtle differences.

For a start, the 'mod cons' included in my new luxurious abode included cushions and curtains and there were also four able seamen to serve as messmen, preparing the meals, waiting at table and keeping the mess clean.

I also had to have a complete change of clothing and was now required to possess three blue suits. Number One suit was made of doeskin and was quite an expensive affair, while Number Two and Three were of serge. Luckily, I had an account with Bernards of Portsmouth and Chatham, who had my measurments and were able to make me the three suits.

My new gear also included three white suits, white socks, shirts and collars and all the necessary accessories associated with my new and more exalted station.

It was, in short, a rather expensive promotion and, although an allowance was made, it did not cover the full cost of being kitted out in a new rig. Anyway, I soon got settled into it – once it arrived from England – and there I was, a Petty Officer, First Class.

Our next port of call was Bermuda, then even more than now, perhaps, the playground of the rich and the hub of the British-controlled Bermudas. It was to be our base for the next three years.

# 22 · Cruise fit for Kings

A clear picture of Bermuda lingers in the memory. There was a dockyard, a hospital, quite a large canteen, a cemetery, a very small naval barracks and a dry dock.

No motor cars were allowed on the island. There were just a few Army personnel and the remainder were Royal Navy.

Across the bay and further inland was the capital, Hamilton, a favourite weekend resort for American businessmen, who brought their secretaries over on the liners *Monarch of Bermuda* and *Queen of Bermuda* for weekends of the good life.

Hamilton, the American playground, was much too expensive for us, but we still managed to have a pretty good time there, that is, when we weren't painting the ship or going out on gunnery or torpedo exercises.

At weekends I would ask the Commander for the second cutter and Stan and his crew would sail away to a little island about twenty miles from the mainland.

This, so we found out, had once been a naval fever centre. It had a tiny natural harbour, just wide enough for the cutter to get in through its protective coral reef which opened up into a nice little bay with a sandy beach.

One or two buildings, which had once been part of the fever hospital, were still standing and, as if to cheer us all up, a small cemetery with graves dating back to the thirteen hundreds.

We would go to our island paradise, taking a picnic, and spend the weekend swimming and sunning ourselves. To us, it was a holiday centre fit for millionaires. Indeed, it could be that you have to be nearly a millionaire these days to swim from that very same beach. Who knows?

We always prepared ourselves for these little holiday excursions, stacking the cutter with provisions, including a good supply of essentials like beer from the canteen.

Once safely installed on our holiday beach, we swam – and I never saw a shark in that bay – and we cooked our food over open fires and, at nights, we had a sing-song around the camp fire before turning in. They were the happy times.

In Bermuda the canteen was some distance from the dockyard – perhaps a mile to a mile and a half – and to get there at night-times we would hire bicycles outside the dockyard gate, for a shilling or so. The canteen was a great place for refreshment, sing-songs, tombola and such forms of entertainment.

Although no motor vehicles of any kind were allowed on the roads, there were one or two carriages, but they were in such short supply that there was very little chance of getting hold of one. The roads were made mainly of coral and would soon wear out under the wheels of vehicles.

To prove, yet again, that variety and sharp contrasts have truly been the spice of my naval life, we set out from the sun drenched Bermudas on a cruise which was to take us to the icy wastes of Northern Canada, the very edge of the Arctic, and back via some of the hottest fleshpots of the USA.

As we steamed steadily north; the weather grew colder and colder. We sailed through the Straits of Belle Isle which separate the island of Newfoundland from Labrador and we visited many northern settlements which were just coming out of their winter 'hibernations'.

Their huts were covered with snow. They had dug paths between houses, shops and the trading posts and they were very glad to see us as we had brought fresh provisions and tinned food.

But our main job on that part of the cruise was to report the position of any icebergs we passed, which could well be a danger to shipping. That was how we came to see the making of an iceberg and what a memorable sight it was, a real example of the power and wonder of nature.

A glacier was sticking out some hundreds of yards into the ocean. Suddenly, with a crack like thunder, it broke and a newborn iceberg went floating away.

These icebergs, in the main, were of tremendous size and, since nine-tenths of each berg was under water, it was easy to understand the danger they represented to shipping.

After spending some time visiting Canada's northern settlements, we came back down through the Belle Isle Strait and way up the St Lawrence River to Montreal where the ship was thrown open to visitors and we had a pretty good time.

Mind you, there was an unusual mishap there which could have been more serious.

We had a new type of foremast made of several layers of moulded three-play. It must have been an untried sort of mast because the cold got into it and then, when we got to Montreal in the sunshine, the heat expanded the moisture and the mast snapped and came crashing down. Nobody was hurt, thank goodness.

But, at least, the top part of the foremast had to be repaired and that was a challenge for the ship's carpenters who had to fashion it from a suitable pole or tree and then fit it.

The ship was open to visitors every afternoon and hundreds came on board to look her over. We entertained many of them in the Petty Officer's mess, showing the ones we fancied around the ship and detailing sailors off to act as guides for the remainder.

This privilege of picking and choosing led to an unexpected disappointment for a man who fancied himself as a bit of a lad with the girls.

I got lucky one day when a pretty girl came my way. Eager to please, I took her to the mess and we had tea and got quite matey.

You may well imagine that I thought my luck was in when she invited me up to her flat next time I was on shore.

Ashore at the next opportunity, you couldn't see Stan for dust as I made tracks for her place. Just as I thought I'd made a conquest, she informed me she was a lesbian and launched into an interesting, if unexpected, history of her life.

In the end, I suppose, I had a certain amount of sympathy for her – maybe even more than I had for myself – but that, as you may well guess, was as far as our relationship ever went.

Three of us Petty Officers, a telegraphist, a yeoman of signals and me had become close friends. In fact, after Montreal – where we went on a moose hunt – we became known as the Three Musketeers (or Mooseketeers, if you like).

There was this chap we met in Montreal who asked if we would like to go moose hunting. Well, it seemed like something else worth a try, so we agreed and got a weekend's leave.

First we travelled by car through the trees and on up the mountain slopes until the wheels could take us no further. Then we took out our provisions and guns and began tracking through the woods to a hut belonging to our guide.

It was beside a lake and, after making ourselves comfortable in the hut and lighting a fire, we went fishing. The trout we caught and cooked that night for supper tasted terrific.

By early morning light the scenery was spectacular, the mountains and forests of Canada, but we were fearless hunters and fearless hunters don't have time to stand around admiring the scenery.

Armed with our guns we went off into the forest. We tracked all day but the most we saw of the moose was their hoof prints. Dead tired, but mighty healthy, we made our way back to the hut that night and slept.

The following day, first thing in the morning, off we went again and this time we did see a moose. We took a shot at it, but just scared it and away it went.

The way that huge animal glided through the forest was a marvel. We did not see him again, or any other moose, for that matter. So, empty handed, we went back to the hut, had a clean up and a shave, trekked back to the car and returned to Montreal. But it had been a good weekend.

There was a more than adequate supply of cabarets in Montreal, all capable of offering the visiting sailors a good time and each very well supplied with hostesses at ten cents a dance.

There was also a brothel which ran parallel to the main street, but several streets further back. The brothel, however, was not so popular because it seemed to contain such a hard-faced bunch of old cows that the sailors were not tempted to bother with them very much.

Instead, they hung around the cabarets, dancing and singing until the early hours and then staggering back to the ship.

That is how we passed our time until we were due to go back down river to Quebec. Time there only to get a quick impression of that French speaking part of Canada and to remember taking tea in the imposing Hotel Fontinec where, in the World War which was still to come, Churchill and Roosevelt were, I believe, to take some of the great decisions which were to change world history.

From Quebec we steamed down the St Lawrence and out to sea, around the coast of Nova Scotia, to drop anchor in Bar Harbour on the coast of Maine.

Bar Harbour seemed to be quite the centre of the yachting fraternity of America. Vastly expensive looking sailing boats took part in some marvellous races.

Money was no object, but the Yanks are not a mean people and they were more than willing to share their good fortune with us Limeys.

They wanted to take us everywhere and it became very much the 'in thing' to have a Limey as a dinner or supper guest.

From Bar Harbour we went on to Boston, a busy city on a river which gave off an awful smell on account of the gas which constantly bubbled up from the river bed. The smell always seemed to be worst in the evenings.

The ship was open to visitors again and we Three Musketeers made contact with a Mr and Mrs Hardcastle. He was an Englishman married to an American and they had grown up daughters.

When they came on board we gave them tea in the Petty Officers' mess and he told me he was the owner of a textile mill. He seemed to be quite a big shot in the town.

Hospitable people, they entertained us quite a lot. We would spend the whole day with them and they would take us to various shows and other attractions. Their large house had more than enough rooms to put us up for the night.

The Hardcastles also had two friends staying with them. I forget their names, but I do recall that he was the owner of the Golden Rod brewery on Long Island, New York.

In Boston on holiday, these visitors accompanied the Hardcastles and we three in quite a few sight-seeing jaunts around the town. They wanted to make sure we did not miss anything that was worth seeing.

After Boston our next port of call was Washington, DC. We went through our normal routine after tying up alongside and opened the ship to visitors. You may guess who were the first four visitors to step on board; Mr and Mrs Hardcastle and their two friends.

They had motored down from Boston, a journey of about a thousand miles, which meant little in a land where journeys are measured in thousands rather than hundreds of miles.

Even so, they must have been pretty keen to show off their country to His Majesty's 'tourists'.

They took us ashore, not just to see the White House and admire all the statues of past American Presidents, but also to tour Washington's high spots and low spots of entertainment.

We had a great time in the American capital and the people of Washington generously opened their hearts to us.

It was impossible to go ashore for a walk. You could only take a few steps before somebody would pull alongside you in a car and offer to take you where-ever you wanted to go, even to their home for a meal.

We were really given the red carpet treatment and enjoyed a right royal time, even after the Hardcastles and their friends left us after three or four days.

After Washington we also had quite a good time in Philadelphia, but my memories of that place are rather different from the joys of the capital city.

Somehow or other – and I shall never know quite how, or why – we found ourselves in an all-male cabaret show. I'd never seen so many poofs in all my life.

They all dressed like girls and spoke like girls, calling each other dearie and darling. It was fun, I suppose, but I've got to admit they gave some jolly good floor shows and you couldn't help laughing at them.

The entertainment was a bit different in another cabaret we visited. There a girl singer had an extraordinarily novel way of getting rich quick. She simply moved around among the patrons lifting her leg over the corner of each table to pick up a ten cent piece without the boring necessity of having to use her hands. It was a talent which we found somewhat unusual and I should imagine the amount of training required to perfect this unconventional skill was well worth the money she earned.

You can be sure we got rid of a good many ten cent pieces!

We stayed in Philadelphia for about two weeks, welcoming visitors on board and having quite a good time on shore.

But soon it was time for us to go back to Bermuda for a refit. It had been a cruise of incredible variety, tremendous interest, great fun and good friendship with the Americans, and thousands of miles of free world travel.

Some people might have paid a fortune for just such a cruise. We got it simply by being in the Royal Navy and part of a ship whose job was to show the flag for the British Empire.

But, even after a cruise fit for kings and millionaires, there was an even better one in store for us after that refit.

# 23 · The Jam Commission

Before we could sample the further delights of world travel, fate took a hand with a tragedy which cost the lives of five good sailors.

We had got back into the routine of our life in Bermuda, visiting the canteen and escaping to our tropical island paradise for weekends of sun and swimming.

Five other sailors had the same object in mind when they set the ship's gig towards another island and sailed off into the blue. That was the last we were to see of them alive for a grisly death awaited them.

A gale blew up during the night and there was not sufficient shelter on the island for the boat so they decided to head back under half sail to the ship.

On the way they hit a reef which was covered at high tide by about four feet of water at most. The boat was smashed against the reef, quickly disintegrating under the pounding of the waves.

The blow was too hard for ship's gigs and mere sailor men, but not for the deadly barracuda fish which swarmed around and ate our five men as they stood on the reef struggling for a foothold. It was a stark choice; death either by drowning or by being eaten alive.

Back on board we knew nothing of this until the search party went out to look for them the following day and found the wreckage of the boat on the reef at low tide and nothing left of our five shipmates save their bones.

In due time our ship completed her refit and we were told we were to go on a cruise to the Pacific. This turned out to be the most interesting cruise I have ever done. It was called the Robinson Crusoe cruise and it was really lovely.

We left Bermuda and headed through the Panama Canal, a marvellous feat of engineering.

Taking a ship through the Panama Canal was – and, I'm sure, still is – an operation of skill and precision and it was all achieved with smooth efficiency and without the shouting of orders through megaphones.

As the ship entered each succeeding lock three hawsers were put aboard each side. The hawsers were held by motors on rails which towed the ship through the lock and held her steady all the way.

In the first lock the ship was raised about thirty feet in less than twenty minutes. It was the same at the second lock; no shouting of orders, just whistle blasts and telephones. It was an amazing feat.

We steamed on through the Canal to the Pacific Ocean and out to sea to visit the uninhabited islands near the trade routes.

The purpose of this was to discover whether any survivors from ships in distress had found their way to the islands since the Royal Navy's previous visit.

When we reached an island, if there were no entrance to the lagoon through its protective reef, we blasted one. Then we went ashore and built a rough hut in which we stowed tinned provisions, fishing lines, fish hooks and gun ammunition, distress rockets and all the things thought to be necessary to maintain life for a year or two.

All this was just in case somebody landed up on the island and was marooned. We would also blaze a trail to the nearest fresh water and leave a notice in the hut warning any shipwrecked mariners about the fruit they could eat and that which they could not.

The animals and birds on these islands, not being accustomed to seeing human beings, were extraordinarily tame. Parrots would come and settle on your shoulder just as if they were in a zoo.

On some islands the population of goats was bigger than need be, while on others there were no goats at all. To even up this imbalance – all in the interests of shipwrecked sailors – we would take two nannies and a billy from an island which had plenty and liberate them on one which had none. There they would be able to breed and thus ensure a supply of fresh meat for any survivors fortunate enough to reach the island.

This was certainly a lovely cruise. As a lover of nature it was wonderful for me to see it 'in the raw', so to speak.

No wonder this patrol was known in the Navy as the 'Jam Commission!'

After calling at all the main islands near the trade routes, we went back to South America and visited the oil stations along the Paraguayan coast. When we called at one for oil, they gave it to us free – I doubt if they could today.

It was fascinating to see the towns which sprang up where oil was discovered. When a new well was found to be capable of producing a good supply of oil a makeshift township would spring up with wooden buildings surrounded by wooden sidewalks.

But when the well ran dry the population would just move on to establish a new town around a new well. All the way down the coast there were 'ghost towns', deserted just as they had been when occupied, and left to rot away in desolation.

The people we found on shore gave us a fine welcome with a dance and a meal. This we greatly appreciated for they lived a hard life in an inhospitable land.

They told us that it hadn't rained in seventeen years. There seemed to be hardly a tree or a shrub, or any piece of greenery, anywhere along that coastline. It is one of the driest places on earth.

I suppose every part of the world has its blessings as well as its problems. Nowhere can be all bad and, in this parched area of the globe, the greatest compensation came in the form of incredible mineral wealth.

Our cruise became almost an educational and geographical exercise as we saw something of the communities dedicated to getting the minerals out of the ground; saltpetre, silver, gold, mercury, almost anything, it seemed to us, that could be imagined.

But it is also true to say that the local people probably did not get a great deal of benefit from this mineral wealth. I do not know who the mine owners were, but the managers were all English and they, and their wives, were all very pleased to see us.

They entertained us on shore and we had a good time visiting the various mines.

I got friendly with one of the mine managers and he gave me two interesting specimens of quartz which I managed to get home safely and still have to this day.

A 'mineral' of a very different type is harvested from the islands we visited on our way down the coast of Chile; guano (concentrated bird droppings).

I have never seen so many sea birds in all my life, birds of all descriptions and natures swarmed around the rocky islands depositing a great white blanket which is a source of fuel and fertiliser. It is the chief way in which this part of the world can conserve energy by using what might best be described as 'natural deposits'.

Guano was, in fact, quite a successful trade and ships left the islands laden with the stuff, to carry it to different countries.

In one place where we went ashore, the guano was up to twelve or fourteen feet deep. The locals would slice it off in huge slabs and store it in their homes and for export.

There were also many thousands of wild duck and our shooting trips would always produce a tremendous 'bag'.

Life was even more hazardous for the little seabirds called Mother Cary's Chicks, most of which would fly out from the land only to be swallowed whole by tremendous gulls before they had reached the safety of the ocean.

Next port of call on our South American tour was Valparaiso, Chile. The first thing I saw as we entered harbour and dropped anchor in the middle of the basin, was the Chilean Navy tied up alongside the outer walls of the mole. I recognised one of the old ships immediately, one we had called the *Canada*. Her Chilean name was *Almirante Latorre*.

Two battleships had been built for the Chilean Navy before the first World War and were not quite finished when war broke out. Britain had, therefore, commandeered them both and used them throughout the war.

They had been quite lovely ships, but they looked a lot different now. They were dirty and untidy, for the Chilean Navy was on strike; and it reminded me of that time back at Invergordon when the Royal Navy went on strike, though our strike had only lasted twenty four hours and I don't suppose, even if it had gone on longer, we would have let our ships get into quite such a bad state.

Valparaiso was a fine and quite large city. In the square on the sea front stood the statue of Captain Pratt, a renegade Englishman, who had had a hand in Chile's struggle for independence early in the nineteenth century.

Many times, on shore, we were asked about Captain Pratt and, with a name like his, you can believe that these well-meaning inquiries produced some ribald answers from us irreverent sailors!

But the local people always seemed satisfied with these answers, remarking that it was very good that we should be acquainted with members of the Pratt family!

The rate of exchange in Valparaiso was terrific. It was almost as good as at Danzig after the First World War when you got a hundred thousand marks to the pound.

In Valparaiso, if you changed two pounds at the bank you would get, in return, enough paper money to fill all your pockets, and you could live in the style of a millionaire.

We were given three days leave to visit the Chilean capital of Santiago and, to get there, we travelled on a magnificent train which ran down the middle of the street.

Way down in South America, these were truly British railways, and, looking back, I remember them as being more modern than the railways of England today – at least, those which serve the country areas.

The trains and carriages were beautifully made. Even the rails and signals had been made by the British.

In Santiago we stayed in quite a good hotel, saw all the sights and then returned to Valparaiso. We liked that city and were determined to make the most of it while we were there.

There was no shortage of social life. The cabarets were plentiful and we got in plenty of singing and dancing, ably assisted by the girls who had left their office jobs as secretaries and typists to come out and help entertain the visiting English sailors.

We were guests in their country and, boy, were they hospitable and eager to make sure we were fully entertained!

From Valparaiso our ship headed for perhaps the world's most famous desert islands, the Chilean islands of Juan Fernandez, which Daniel Defoe immortalised as the scene of the Robinson Crusoe story.

Proof that there had once been a real life Robinson Crusoe – a Scottish sailor called Alexander Selkirk who had been put ashore there and forgotten – was still to be seen in the cave where he had lived and his look-out perch.

Much more recently, this island had been the scene of a First World War action involving the German light cruiser *Dresden*.

After being damaged in battle she had put in and started repairs. The German sailors had set up guns ashore.

But the *Dresden* was discovered and shelled by the British Fleet and her crew put up quite a fight before they could all be rounded up.

We found the islands populated and supporting a thriving crab and lobster industry exporting canned lobsters all over the world.

We went ashore and made the laborious climb up to 'Robinson Crusoe's' look-out point, which was marked by a stone slab. We also visited the cave where his crude cooking and domestic implements were still preserved.

There was also a statue looking out over the spot where the *Dresden* had been sunk only a few years earlier. It was an impressive memorial to the German sailors who had died in the fighting there.

'Robinson Crusoe's' island was the last, and one of the most exotic, calls of our fascinating tour down South America's Pacific Coast.

We headed North again, back through the Panama Canal – with a few days' leave in Panama City – and returned to Bermuda.

So ended a cruise during which we had travelled 11,000 miles and seen a whole new world in which hard reality, romance and fantasy were all mixed to leave memories which can never fade.

# 24 · Polishing up the Police

Even people on world cruises have to get down to doing the chores now and again, and in the Royal Navy the chores meant cleaning and painting the ship, doing gunnery and torpedo tests and other exercises.

That is how we spent most of our time back in Bermuda but it wasn't long before we were off on our travels again. This time it was to be a Caribbean cruise to the Windward and Leeward Islands.

We had been to North America and South America and now we were on the third stage of a sort of marathon commission which was not unusual in those days but which would not happen today, when sailors tend not to be away for more than about nine months at a time.

Our first stop this time was at the island of Dominica in the Leeward Islands.

We had time to go ashore for a look around and do a bit of fishing before, one day, not long after our arrival, the Captain sent for me. He asked; 'How would you like to sail to our next destination in the cutter?'

I jumped at the idea. Our next destination was to be St Lucia and what sailor worth his salt could resist the invitation of a sail in those waters?

Preparing to leave three days before the ship sailed, we provisioned the cutter which was manned by a volunteer crew – no difficulty in getting volunteers – which included a midshipman. We also had a portable wireless.

The trade winds in that area are usually favourable so we didn't have much sail manipulation or tacking to do, but could set a straight course.

We fished and sang songs and sunned ourselves, getting so brown we could later have been mistaken for native Caribbean inhabitants. We swanned along, really living the life of Reilly, and enjoying ourselves immensely.

About half-way to St Lucia our ship came up alongside us. More provisions were passed into the cutter and considerate inquiries were made as to our health and wellbeing. They needn't have worried, we were well away.

After our arrival at St Lucia and, promptly after my return to the ship, I was called into the Captain's cabin. When this happens you tend to cast around in your mind to see if you've done anything wrong, but the Skipper had a job for me, and a pretty demanding one it was, too.

I was to visit the various islands in the Windward and Leeward groups to teach the local police things like rifle drill, revolver and rifle firing, mob drill, and how to cover each other in street fighting.

It didn't take me long to find out that this was going to be a lovely job.

I started by spending three weeks in St Lucia, working at the police station and living in quite a nice hotel.

There was a social side to my life too as I was entertained by the local head man as well as by the representative of the British Crown.

The St Lucia Police of that time couldn't have been a finer or more helpful body of men. They were very keen to learn and were all true Britishers at heart. Their King and Queen were our King and Queen and they wanted everyone to know it.

One chap, although he kept his revolver nicely oiled and clean, had never fired it and was half scared of it. But after he got the hang of how to use it, he became quite efficient.

From St Lucia I went on to Barbados, an island with a much larger population, mostly in its capital, Bridgetown. Not surprisingly, the Police Force was a good deal larger than that at St Lucia.

But I was again well received and billeted in a good hotel. When not busy training the police, I was again entertained by the local inhabitants, including the white community.

There was quite a big white population, mostly attached to the sugar industry and, apart from being a bit snobbish, they treated me fairly well; but not, I may say, half as warmly as the black people did.

Next, I was on my way back to Dominica, but by a form of transport not entirely to be expected in the Royal Navy. If my ship was unable to pick me up at one island and deposit me at another, I had to take passage in a banana boat.

I visited the police forces in all the main islands in turn and I have never met a finer crowd of men to train. They were absolutely one hundred per cent keen.

I eventually caught up with the ship at Jamaica and became, once again, a member of the ship's company.

From Jamaica, we went on to Venezuela, a country with a small fleet which had been bought from the British. They wanted twelve volunteers from the ship's company to teach the Venezuelan sailors and their officers how to run the ships.

The rate of pay they were offering was, for those times, terrific. Something like one pound a day was a really good income.

I volunteered, needless to say, but this time I was not so lucky. They soon had their twelve volunteers anyway and they became, for the time being, members of the Venezuelan Navy.

Next country on our world cruise itinerary was Mexico and I recall travelling up by train to Mexico City where there was a festival.

We had organised a game of football with a local team. We played in the afternoon, the score, I recall, was 1–1 and it was quite a good hard fought game.

Then we were entertained by the Mexican Government that evening. The festival was in full swing. There was a great deal of revelry and we British sailors were treated like real VIPs with a banquet in our honour.

I was reminded of our visit to Mexico City when, rather more recently, the Olympic Games were held in that country. The competitors then – and in the World Cup soccer finals – complained that the altitude affected their game.

Well, I don't recall that it had any effect on us. We played our afternoon game of football and lived it up pretty well in the evening without suffering any after effects.

And we were still fit enough the following morning for the train journey back to our ship after a tremendous twenty-four hours in Mexico City.

The last leg of another great cruise took us back to Bermuda. The whole purpose of these cruises was to 'show the flag' and, in those days of Empire, when British sailors were welcomed with open arms almost wherever they went, showing the flag could be great fun.

Our time in Bermuda was really just an interlude between our jaunts and we occupied ourselves with the usual chores and refit, which is just where I came in at the beginning of this chapter.

# 25 · Monster – or Mystery?

There can be only one thing that is more impressive and memorable than seeing one of New York's traditional Broadway ticker tape welcomes for returning heroes; and that is actually being one of the 'heroes' welcomed.

It is an honour which happens to very few people and on very special occasions after which those involved can feel privileged to be able to say;'I was there'.

The annual Broadway celebrations which had greeted the end of the First World War are now part of history, but this year the scene is as vivid in my memory as if it had just happened last week. I shall never forget it because I was literally in the thick of it.

New York City was, in fact, the first port of call on our next cruise and what an impressive sight it was as we passed the Statue of Liberty on Bedloe's Island and saw the immense city unfold in front of us.

Everywhere, skyscrapers reached for the clouds. Yet amid all this splendour my first experience was of meeting old friends and being made to feel at home.

The reason was that we had not been in New York twenty-four hours before Mr and Mrs Hardcastle and the people from the Golden Rod Brewery turned up.

We went ashore with them, first visiting the top of the Woolworth's Building – then the tallest in New York – where you could make a small plastic record to send off by letter to the folks back home. To us it just seemed another of the remarkable new inventions which seemed to abound in America.

We, also, went over to the Statue of Liberty, climbing the winding staircase which goes up the inside of her upraised arms and leads into the torch of liberty itself.

In one of the New York cabarets we visited the five dollar cover charge included drinks and the cabaret performance. If you wanted food, or anything costing more than the five dollars, you were charged later when you left the cabaret.

We were in New York – and lucky to be there – when the Armistice was signed and the celebrations quickly got under way.

Not like the more restrained celebrations in England – where we matelots might have been expected to attend sombre church thanksgiving services – the Broadway ticker tape parade was a riot and an experience to be savoured for a lifetime afterwards.

We were placed in open cars festooned with the Union Jack and the White Ensign. In these colourful and patriotic vehicles we were driven through the city to a welcome fit for kings and presidents.

The climax to our triumphant tour was the journey down Broadway where, from the windows high up on the buildings, a storm of ticker-tape descended. It was thicker than a snowstorm.

There was paper, ticker-tape and anything in the paper line that the people could lay their hands on. The ground was a foot deep in paper and the crowds gave us a tremendous rousing reception.

The noise was deafening. You would have thought we had won the war on our own instead of simply being a few friendly allies lucky enough to be in the right place at the right time.

We finished up at the famous Waldorf Hotel where the New Yorkers treated us to a slap up dinner and dance. It was a really impressive affair and we were the guests of honour.

Afterwards, I was fascinated to see a sight which was almost as staggering as the ticker-tape storm itself – the clear-up operation.

First a police car came along the street, sounding its siren, and I noticed that passers-by, especially the women, began to dive into shop doorways and keep out of the way. It was easy to tell that they must know something I didn't.

The reason for their evasive action was that behind the police car came a large vehicle which was, in effect, a huge vacuum cleaner.

Paper lay thick on the road and festooned the walls, window ledges, telegraph poles and every imaginable nook and cranny. But so fierce was the suction created by the vacuum car that all the paper was lifted up and engulfed by the machine which, as it passed down the road, seemed to be followed by a thick cloud. No wonder the passers-by sought refuge and the women clung to their skirts for the suction must have been terrific.

For us three friends there followed an experience which, I suppose, we would all remember for very different reasons than the ticker-tape welcome.

We went to the Golden Rod Brewery and celebrated not wisely but too well. We had a wonderful time, sampling all the different types of beer and getting into quite a merry state up in the office.

By the time Mrs Hardcastle and friends appeared on the scene to see what had happened we were hardly fit for civilised company, laughing, joking, maybe even singing, but certainly extremely well oiled.

They gave us each a dose of something they called bromide. What it was I don't know, but with that and a cup of black coffee we were as sober as judges within half an hour – and ready to start the rounds again!

The rate of exchange in New York wasn't too bad, I think it was five dollars, seventy five cents to the pound, and that makes you pause for thought when you hear of the exchange rates today.

A visit to New York would not be complete without a trip over the Brooklyn Bridge, to the Bronx area.

I say it wouldn't be complete because – in those days anyway – it was only by visiting the Bronx that you could see how New York was a city of two halves; the magnificent skyscrapers and the Waldorf Hotel on the one hand and the squalor and filth of poverty on the other.

In the Bronx, you had to kick your way through the refuse in the streets. It was the sort of place where the police walked in pairs on patrol for their own safety.

We stayed in New York for about two weeks before sailing on to Baltimore where we had the usual good time and were well entertained on shore by the local people.

From Baltimore we went to Philadelphia and then back through the Panama Canal down to Valparaiso again. The rate of exchange was still good and we had a jolly fine time there.

On the way back we saw spectacular evidence of the grim side of nature, a life and death struggle at sea.

A school of whales had come into the warmer water to give birth to their young. It is at that time, when carrying and actually giving birth, that whales are vulnerable to sharks as they are unwieldy and can't thrash about much.

If the pun can be excused, scores and scores of sharks were having a whale of a time and the poor old whales could do nothing, it seemed, to defend themselves.

The sea ran red with blood as the sharks inflicted terrible slaughter. But there was nothing we could do, as we simply steamed on.

Mind you, we did a fair bit of our own kind of fishing and we caught several decent sized swordfish. They gave pretty good sport, because you would have to play them for quite a time on a light line before you could bring them in for the kill.

We used to have these as a meal and I rather liked them. The flesh was firm, not flaky like the fish to which we are accustomed in this country, but solid like chunks of meat.

We called at several ports on the Colombian coast, where there was not much action to be had ashore, and then we went back through the Panama Canal and down to Barbados.

We did quite a lot of fishing and it was there that we hooked our mystery monster; something so huge and powerful that it seemed capable of towing a ship.

The mystery happened one day when we were fishing with an ordinary cod line and a large hook. It was our normal practice to start off with a light line, catch a small fish to use as bait on a larger line, and gradually work our way up in that way.

I caught what we called an amber fish, maybe two or three feet long, attached him to a large hook and let him swim down.

Almost immediately I knew I had hooked something really big.

We couldn't hold on to the cod line. We let it play out through our hands until we came almost to the end. Then we made it fast to the guard rail.

It stretched and stretched like a piece of cotton until, finally, it snapped.

We knew there was something tremendous down there so the next day we got a shark hook and baited it with a large lump of meat that had got a bit high. Then we fixed the hook and meat to the fog buoy wire which, measuring about a quarter of an inch in diameter, had a breaking strain of up to five tons.

We rove it through a block on the end of the cutter's davits, and lowered the hook down into the water.

It wasn't long before we hooked this monster and off it went. We tried to hold it on the brake of the drum that held the wire, but the brake wasn't strong enough and got red hot.

We had to pour buckets of water over the brake to try to hold and keep it intact. But the wire ran right out to the end and we all scattered.

The wire snapped, came inboard writhing and whipping like something that was itself alive, creating havoc, knocking down stanchions and, if it had caught anybody, it would have taken off their legs and arms.

We never did find out what we had hooked that day in Barbados. Our mystery monster made off, but not before, in our one-sided struggle, it had pulled the anchored ship right round to windward.

That fish, monster, whatever it was must have been a giant among fish. We didn't have a chance to go after him again because we sailed the next day to steam the long haul right up to Newfoundland.

There we saw a wonderful sight. I think it was at St John's where the river was absolutely full to overflowing with salmon. They were making their way up river, over the falls, to spawn. There were so many that those on the edges were being pushed up the river banks to die.

There was a company at St John's which specialised in exporting young salmon around the world. At intervals they would haul out some fish, squeeze the eggs from them into large troughs and then return the fish to the water.

They would then mix the eggs up in the troughs by hand, then dish the mixture out into trays which would be taken away to the firm's hatcheries.

When the little fish had reached the right size they would transfer them to various rivers around the world and, where-ever they went, these young salmon would somehow find their way back to St John's in about five years time and would go up the river to spawn.

There was also a factory from which canned salmon could be bought for sixpence a tin. I should think that price, from a time when a penny was still worth something, hardly covered the cost of the tin itself, let alone its contents.

We did our share of fishing during a cruise around the island. In a bay where we anchored I have never seen so many flat fish in all my life. You only had to put your hook over the side and you caught one for they seemed quite prepared to take a bite at anything. With tubs and tubs of flat fish on board, fish and chips was bound to be on the supper menu.

Perhaps I shall always remember this cruise as the cruise of the fish, because they figured largely in our lives wherever we went, the whales, the sharks, swordfish, salmon, flat fish – and our mysterious monster.

Newfoundland was the last destination before we returned to Bermuda having clocked up a mammoth 13,000 miles on that cruise alone.

# 26 · Homeward Bound

Revisiting places that have already made a profound impression on you is not always a happy experience. How often, it seems, has time dealt unkindly with places, as well as people, of fond memory.

Nowhere could have proved this point in a more spectacularly desolate way than Para, the once bustling industrial community which had temporarily been base for our earlier eventful and ill-fated expedition deep into the Amazon jungle in search of the explorer, the story of which I have already told.

Para, about sixty miles up the Amazon River, was the first port of call on our next cruise out of Bermuda; and what a contrast I found.

The sight which greeted our eyes was pitiful. Where once people had earned their livings from river-borne industry and commerce, Para was now a ghost town rapidly being reclaimed by the jungle which surrounded it. The jibs of the big cranes on the wharfs were rusted through and the cranes had toppled, some into the river and others on to the wharf itself.

With the end of the rubber boom, the town seemed to have been abandoned, just as it stood. It was as if somebody had given an order and all life in Para had stopped in one split second; a moment frozen in time. But time, and the jungle, do not stand still.

Even the trams stood deserted in the derelict streets, just where they had dropped their last passengers. And the jungle was returning to claim its own. Vines, trees and bushes were growing everywhere, through the trams, along the tracks, in the streets, on the pavements and in the buildings.

The place was absolutely deserted, apart from a few negro families who were squatting in one or two of the habitable buildings.

I went into a church which had once been quite an impressive building. To get in, I had to force my way through the vines which festooned the doorway.

Inside, everything had been left as it had been when the church was in use. The pews were still there but the undergrowth had grown

116

through and round them in such profusion that we could only just recognise what they were and that they were still there.

The altar was still in position, but the altar cloth had been so eaten away by insects that it hung in threads. The organ had half collapsed and some of the organ pipes lay scattered about the church.

Today, all these years later, if the jungle has been allowed to continue the process of obliteration unchecked, I doubt if any traces of that once lively city remain. Even then the place was well and truly dead and quickly being swallowed up by the jungle from whence it had sprung. Nothing more than the sad echo of a former life.

From Para we went on down the coast, stopping at most of the principle towns and cities until we reached Rio. I will draw a veil over the two weeks we spent there, largely because I have already described an earlier visit in detail.

This time, Rio was chiefly memorable for the fact that we were there when news came of the approaching end of our American Commission. In six weeks time we were to head for our home port of Chatham to pay the ship off.

We received the news with mixed feelings. It was good to be going home and we had a spell of leave to look forward to with our families, but it had been a wonderful two and a half years Commission, full of adventure, travel and incident. The chance of a lifetime to see the world and build up memories which have warmed me on many a cold night since.

Everybody in the ship had behaved on shore with the best of good manners and I think our cruise around this part of the world to 'show the flag' had done British prestige a lot of good.

On leaving Rio we went back up to Bermuda to take on stores and prepare for our journey home. Travelling with us were one or two ratings from other ships taking passage home.

Then, finally, we set sail, flying our paying off pennant and saying a fond farewell to the Americans and the West Indies. From the far north of Canada to the depths of the Amazon jungle and far down the west coast of South America, we had met people, made friends and seen sights that would remain with us for ever.

From the excitement of a New York ticker-tape parade to the humid vastness of the Amazon forest; from the beaches of Bermuda to the eerie isolation of Robinson Crusoe's Island, we would all have experiences to remember, mariners' tales to tell our grandchildren.

Yet, after eight leisurely days of steaming across the Atlantic we saw another sight which had warmed the hearts of generations of Englishmen before us and would move the spirit of many more after us; the white cliffs of Dover.

We sailed out of the Channel and into Chatham Dockyard, our pennant proudly flying from a weary old warhorse that had taken us safely thousands of miles and was now due for a well earned rest and refit.

For us, her ship's company, all that remained was the journey home to a reunion with our families and to recount just some of the adventures of our cruise fit for kings.

# 27 · A Girl Called Laura

When I got back from HMS *York* there was to be, though I didn't know it at the time, a reunion that would set me on a firm and steady course for the rest of my life.

The popular idea of a sailor is that he has a girl in every port. That isn't always true, and, even if it was, I don't think I would be too eager to admit it in print.

What is true is that Jack usually tries to enjoy himself wherever he goes around the world and I had been no exception to the general rule.

There had been plenty of visits to foreign ports, expeditions to all-night cabarets and the 'fleshpots' of the world and I had enjoyed my fair share of drinking bouts both abroad and at home.

But there comes a time when every chap has to settle down a bit and there was, back at Beccles, a girl who was going to help me do just that.

Up to now I had hardly noticed her; this girl called Laura. I had been friendly with her parents for some years and I had seen her as a child. A child who – I might say, if it doesn't sound too big-headed – seemed to dote on me. She would clean my shoes, polish my medals, run errands for me. She seemed to think the world of me.

That was before I had gone away to America in HMS *York*. For three years we corresponded and, at first, I read with interest that she and another sailor were courting.

But they quarrelled and, as time went on, our letters became more and more friendly. And when I returned from the *York* what a change had come over the seventeen-year-old girl I had left.

She was now a young lady, out at work in a shop, pretty as ever, and still – thank heavens – kindly disposed towards me.

We got engaged before I went back to the Navy. Serving on board HMS *Velox* – and in charge of twenty men who were doing repair work and putting destroyers into 'mothballs' – I found myself in a nice 'cushy' job just at the time I needed to be.

While I was there Laura and I decided to get married and, after the wedding at Beccles, we lived in 'digs' in the centre of the town at The Walk.

This arrangement didn't work out too well so we moved to stay with an old friend of Laura's in London Road where we stayed some time.

Eventually I was able to move Laura down to Gillingham, in Kent, so that we could be together. I was able to see her much more often, every time, in fact, that I had a spare moment and my leave was good.

She wasn't in Gillingham long before I got my next sea-going draft, but I wasn't too worried because I only had about six months to do in the Royal Navy so I knew our separation would not be for long.

However, it was to be an unhappy time, both for me and Laura; a time which produced only one noticeably happy event in the arrival of our first child.

# 28 · An Unhappy Ship

Nowadays, through television, thousands of people are able, each year, to share something of the excitement and sheer sweaty physical exertion of the Royal Navy Field Gun Run.

For weeks before the Royal Tournament the teams from Chatham, Portsmouth and Devonport build up their fitness training and speed for the exhausting series of contests which go on through the period of the tournament.

In my day, the competition was no less fierce for want of the spotlight of television. In fact, I would guess the competition for places in the gun crews was even tougher than it is today.

After my spell of leave I had found myself back in the gunnery school at Chatham, back in the old routine of officers before breakfast and classes after.

Being chosen as one of the instructors for the field gun run was a heaven sent opportunity to escape that old routine, but I soon found that the job of selecting the Chatham team was not as easy as you would think.

There must have been quite a hundred volunteers, for places in the team were popular. We instructors had quite a job selecting two guns' crews.

The men not only had to be strong but also wiry, fit and tough enough to take a few hefty knocks.

We started the training course on a bit of spare land and rigged up the familiar obstacles, measured it all out and started off in slow motion.

Inevitably, we had quite a number of casualties at the start. One chap lost his grip on a wheel going across the traverse gear, the wheel fell on him and broke two or three ribs.

There were several minor accidents before we eventually got two crews together, with about six reserves, and we started proper training.

Finally, we went up to Olympia and competed in the gun run itself, and, I am pleased to say, that we won the competition. We took the cup back to Chatham and it was the first time it had been won there for quite a number of years.

I was getting on now in the Service and had only eighteen months to do before completing my time for pension, so I applied for a vocational training course.

The idea of the course was to give people who were nearing their naval pension some experience of life and a trade outside the Service.

You had to do a bit of paper-hanging, house decorating, brick laying (with an experienced builder), cement mixing and things like that.

I also went into the dockyard to do a bit of copper smithing, making pipes and so on. There was some instruction, too, on the work of an electrician. A short course revealed some of the mysteries of house wiring and many of the jobs associated with electrical apparatus.

The whole course lasted, I suppose, about three months. It was really designed for people who had only about six months to do for pension. But my journey towards a pension was not going to be as simple as that. I still had some seagoing service to get in. It came with a new draft to a brand new ship, the 8-inch gun cruiser, HMS *Southampton*.

I joined the ship at Plymouth and it didn't take long through the commissioning and the usual shake-down trials to find out she was not a happy ship.

The Commander, who earned himself the nickname of 'Mousy', seemed to me to be just about the most inefficient officer I have ever come across in the whole of my experience in the Royal Navy.

He was one of those obstinate men who think they know everything yet give every indication they know nothing.

Every manoeuvre when you were with the Fleet was an evolution, a competition against the other ships. It was recognised that your ship had to be the first, and the best, whenever a signal was received from the Flagship.

We hadn't a hope. Our Commander slipped up on everything, and we were lumbered every time, the last ship to complete every manoeuvre.

For instance, the relatively simple job of spreading the quarterdeck awning presented major problems. We know it wasn't an easy job in this ship because the wire jackstay stood about twelve to fifteen feet high on the deck and to get the awning over this was quite difficult.

I suggested that we crowsfoot a rope into the centre of the awning, lay it up through a block on the main mast and hoist the entire awning up clear of the turret.

Before it was hoisted it would be folded, concertina fashion, with the ear-ring attached so that all one had to do was to haul out on the ear-rings, break the yarns that were holding the folds and the awning would automatically spread.

He would have none of this, until the sailmaker complained that he couldn't repair the awning much more. So he resigned himself to changing his ideas a bit.

Even then, instead of folding the awning concertina fashion, he rolled it up, which made it a solid lump hanging in mid-air.

There were so many minor things that spoiled the harmony of the ship. Hoisting a cutter was another example of the way we managed to do everything wrong. The falls were rove laboriously around the ship so that it took the entire ship's company to hoist the cutter. We had to clear lower deck and, invariably, this was done during the meal hour.

Dinner hour, for a sailor, was normally regarded as well nigh sacred and it was an unwritten rule that he should not be disturbed during it, unless this was absolutely unavoidable.

The sailor would spend the first half-hour at his meal and the second, getting his head down on a makeshift pillow, and having his after-dinner siesta.

The fact that the Commander invariably timed cutter drill to break into this sacred hour did nothing to improve his already rock-bottom popularity and worsened the discontent in the ship.

It was customary for a warning to be sounded five minutes before 'hands fall in' after meals. The idea of this was to allow time for the sailors to stow away their pillows, or whatever they had been using as head rests, so that the messdecks were left tidy.

The Commander put a stop to this. The result was that, when 'hands fall in' was sounded everybody scrambled up topside leaving their pillows where they were, on stools or tables.

'Mousy' promptly complained about untidy messdecks and punished the men concerned, which, not surprisingly, made him even more unpopular.

It was at this time that the Spanish Civil War broke out and we were detailed to patrol the Spanish coast to stop gun-running, pick up refugees and generally be helpful.

It was to be yet another adventure in my life at sea and because of the unsettled state of the world at the time, I was none too keen to let my wife know exactly where I was serving.

As it happened, she had enough on her mind at the time, having our first child, without having to worry whether Stan had managed to get himself back in the firing line. So I made arrangements with a chum of mine in barracks that I would send him my letters home and he would post them on from Chatham.

I put all my letters in two envelopes, the outer one addressed to my mate in Chatham and the inner one to my wife at home.

I think it worked quite well. Although the *Southampton* was mentioned several times on the BBC News, I don't think my wife ever caught on.

Life was quite busy off the Spanish coast. It wasn't too easy trying to stop merchant ships that were attempting to run the gauntlet attracted by the huge prices being paid for arms and ammunition.

The refugees were even more of a problem. They were coming out from the shore in all types of boats, some quite small, others large. There were steam driven boats, sailing boats, rowing boats, almost every type of craft imaginable.

The sea there on the fringe of the Bay of Biscay is always fairly rough and always has quite a deep swell. We had quite a job getting the refugees on board.

We put scrambling nets over the side and, those who could, struggled up them and into the ship. Others were hoisted inboard with ropes and cradles rigged up to lift the younger children on board.

My job was to search all the refugees as they came aboard and remove any arms or knives which they may have concealed around their bodies. This was quite a big job and I soon had a large collection of all types of revolvers, pistols and knives. Some were antiquated and would have made fine exhibits in a museum, but others were quite modern.

The collection was stowed away in the steerage flats under lock and key every evening after we had got the last of the day's refugees on board.

We gave them all a hot meal and drinks and, when we had two or three hundred of them on board we would take them to a point just above Gibraltar. There we had to leave them in refugee camps.

We spent most of our time picking up refugees or closed up at action stations because there was a Spanish cutter in the area and nobody knew whose side she was on. The sky was also pretty full of aircraft.

From the information we gathered from the refugees, we got the impression that there must have been a horrible slaughter on shore. Franco was having German and Italian help and both these nations were intent on trying out their latest weapons with disastrous results for the population.

Luckily, after about three weeks of this, the Civil War moved away from the area we had been detailed to patrol and things gradually seemed to return to normal.

I think the war moved further down into the Mediterranean area around Barcelona, but that was not our pigeon. It was the responsibility of the Mediterranean Fleet.

But my time with the *Southampton* had given me one gloriously happy moment. Our daughter, Pauline, had been born just after the Spanish Civil War when the ship lay in Weymouth harbour.

That fact had enabled me to catch a train heading homewards to Beccles straight away to arrive home at midnight and to meet, and greet, my little daughter.

Though sailors spend much time away from home, they are often devoted family men, and it was to be the great pleasure of my life that my daughter, Pauline, was to be followed over the next eight years by two sons, Ralph and Trevor.

So, we went back to Chatham and gave our normal fourteen days' leave. We had been in Commission for a year and, as it was customary in the Royal Navy, we mustered to be handed our papers and told how our performance had been assessed for that year.

My assessment gave me a bit of a shock. I was reckoned to be 'satisfactory'.

That may sound all right, but I had received 'exceptional's' in pretty well every ship I had been in up to date and 'satisfactory' just didn't seem to me to be anything like good enough.

The Commander must have read my mind and seen there my opinion of him.

It was no good complaining. Once your papers were marked they were marked and there was nowt you could do about it.

All things considered, it was a pretty good job my relief came on board two days before the ship was due to set sail again and I was free to do my vocational training.

Nobody was more pleased than me to see the back of HMS *Southampton* for she had been, for me, an unhappy ship.

# 29 · The Ten-Day Postman

As an ex-Royal Navy man I know I belong to a kind of privileged 'club'. But my particular club is pretty exclusive because I am one of those sailors who actually left the Navy twice.

Mind you, I didn't feel particularly privileged the first time because I spent six weeks on the dole and only ten days in a civilian job before, with the Second World War looming up, the Navy came to its senses and realised it just couldn't do without Stan.

Before leaving the Navy the first time I went on quite a good vocational course.

Working each day from nine in the morning to four in the afternoon, my first adventure was to the Carpenter's shop where we were taught how to use the tools and make joints.

I made a toolchest first, for myself, and then I made a 'dumb waiter' which I still have to this day.

Second port of call on our course was with the bricklayer who showed us how to lay bricks, make foundations, mix cement and make things like the bird bath which was my pride and joy. We also did private jobs out in the town.

From there, we went into the coppersmith's shop in the dockyard and were taught how to fashion copper. I must admit I was rather pleased with my efforts in making a copper kettle for myself. I also produced a couple of ashtrays.

Next we were to be instructed by the electricians who initiated us into the mysteries of house wiring and how dynamos and batteries worked.

Interior decorating was the next skill we were to learn, how to hang paper, apply plaster, paper ceilings and so on. Also varnishing, graining and how to use paint brushes properly.

Again, our newly learned skills were much in demand for doing jobs in private houses whose owners would pay a reasonable fee for their interior decorating. It was quite an interesting course.

Next in our voyage of vocational training was the plumber's shop where we were taught how to sweat a joint, how the various cisterns worked and how to re-adjust them.

In all, the course took nearly three months and I was very pleased indeed that I had done it. You never knew when the skills we had picked up would come in handy for finding a job after leaving the Navy.

I only had a month to go before being pensioned off. I wasn't given any classes but just odd jobs in the gunnery school, taking a class now and again if the instructor was sick or absent for some other reason.

Finally, the day came when I had to see the Doctor and the Paymaster and prepare to leave the Navy with a pension and twenty-eight days' leave to my credit. If it seemed little enough, at the time, after all the adventures of a long and varied seafaring life, I wasn't to know that within a few weeks I would be back in uniform again.

For the moment, here I was, home at Beccles on twenty-eight days' leave – leading to what I thought would seem like an endless leave – with my wife and daughter who was just a few months old.

In the first week we went visiting to Yarmouth, Gorleston and Lowestoft. The second week I did a bit of gardening – a seafarer getting his land legs, you might say.

Our large garden included quite a big lawn and, as I didn't have a lawnmower, I had to cut it with a pair of shears. There was also the hedge to trim, the garden to dig and the vegetables to plant. I kept busy.

After my twenty-eight days expired there was no work of any kind. There was me, a sailor newly skilled in the arts of home decorating, carpentry and plumbing and not a job to be had.

We were going through a depression and quite a lot of people were on the dole. 'Signing on' was one of the unhappiest moments of my life, especially after such an active time at sea.

I could well understand how people may feel discarded, like a non-returnable bottle, after leading a life of travel and service in the King's Forces.

I suppose I was one of the luckier ones. I was only on the dole for about six weeks, but the money wasn't all that good and, with my pension, we could only just about make ends meet.

I had applied for two or three jobs and then, to my surprise, one of them suddenly turned up. I was to be interviewed to be a postman. There were three applicants and we had to go before a board who decided our fate.

I was the lucky one and was chosen to start work the following day.

My money was to be £4. 10s (four pounds ten shillings) a week, just a little bit more than I had been receiving on the dole.

But for the second time in my life, the rumours of world war were gathering force and I hadn't been a postman for more than ten days when my recall came through to rejoin the Navy.

I had kept most of my uniform, so I didn't need much kitting out. I made my farewells and reported back to Chatham Barracks. I was immediately drafted to Sheerness, to the ROAB, which was a rifle course and shooting range.

One of the best things about this drafting was that I managed to get 'digs' ashore and my wife and daughter were able to join me at Sheerness. But we hadn't been there long before war was formally declared and things began to get started.

Have you ever had the feeling that you are going through it all for the second time round. I had as I dug the air raid shelter in the back garden for my wife and daughter and our landlady and as all my colleagues at the ROAB got drafted to other jobs until I was left there in sole charge.

Here was Stan – older, yes; wiser, perhaps; but still in the Royal Navy and still, somehow, caught up in the action.

# 30 · Commandos and Close Shaves

The Second World War found me right at the heart of the job of training and producing efficient fighting men.

At first, they were just in classes on the rifle range. Then, as the war really began to get going, I was transferred to the anti-aircraft establishment down on the point. This was a much better place. The buildings were better and there was more scope all round for the training work.

We continued with exercises and practice on the rifle range and then branched out into something new; Commando training.

For these classes men came from all the Navy's various depots around the country, from Lowestoft, from Chatham, from Portsmouth and Devonport.

We also entertained a smattering of Army people and a few RAF types. We got on pretty well with the 'Pongos' and the fly boys, possibly partly because of the highly undesirable and uncomfortable things we had to ask them to endure.

I had a staff of ten instructors and we had to map out a course which would create, as nearly as possible, the sort of conditions the Commandos would meet on the battlefield.

First they had to embark in a boat and approach the course along a moat which led to a fearsome looking sheet of iron which they had to scale.

The way to do this was to throw a grappling iron up to the top and then climb up the rope and over the top. It may sound like a simple enough exercise for a fit man, but these chaps were each weighed down with a full pack, helmet and rifle. And, in any case, this was just the start.

On reaching the top of the iron sheet they had to go across a 'chasm', hand over hand along a wire until they reached the other side.

Then, across two narrow planks, then through a tunnel which had barbed wire inside, then over several ditches and other obstacles set up all along the course.

All the time they had to concentrate on the accuracy of their own rifle marksmanship, firing as they reached the 600, 500, 400, 200 and 100 yards points along the course.

Finally, they had to fix bayonets and charge at dummies placed at the end of the course.

Easy? It might have been, if it hadn't been for the fact that the people on the course were, all the while, being hampered by marksmen firing rifles close to them and by the sudden and unexpected concussion of thunder flashes and electrically controlled explosives erupting uncomfortably close by and spewing earth and stones all over them.

How do you keep going and keep your rifle fire accurate when you are running through a smoke screen? That was the sort of test we had to put these British servicemen through, making their surroundings as much like a real battlefield as possible.

Our training school was very much a going concern, with as many as one hundred men arriving each Monday to do a week's training.

For Stan, a man accustomed to action, this meant quite a lot of paperwork, with draft notices to be made out for every man arriving or leaving. They had to be fed, paid and allotted their rum ration and, it all involved a good deal of organisation.

Things went fairly smoothly despite the fact that we were constantly harrassed by air raids which got very hectic at times, both by day and at night.

The German aircraft would come over and machine gun us during the day and return with bombs at night.

In the Thames estuary and at Sheerness, we had quite a large anti-aircraft battery and if the German planes were discouraged from going on to London they would drop their bombs on us. Several fell in the compound but, luckily, nobody was killed.

That doesn't mean we didn't have some pretty narrow escapes and, as you might guess, I had one of the narrowest. This seems totally in character for a man who had already had more narrow escapes in his naval life than Houdini.

One day, I happened to be at the foot of a flight of steps when a bomb fell and blew me up them. Almost immediately, another landed nearby and blew me back down again.

To say that I was a bit shaken is probably an understatement. In fact, I was so weak that, when I had a cup of coffee in my hand, I had to tie a scarf to my wrist and then put it round my neck in order to pull my hand, and the cup, to my mouth to drink.

Anyhow, I soon got over that little escapade and was fit enough to be riding a bike when I had my next unexpected brush with the enemy.

I had been down to the dockyard bank to draw some money – I had to pay the men if their pay-day occurred during the week they were on the range – and I was biking back along the Esplanade when, suddenly, I saw a plane coming straight down the sea front.

Instinct made me leap off the bike. No sooner had I taken cover under the Esplanade than a stream of tracer bullets ripped right down the centre of the road along which I had just been cycling, setting fire to the tarmac in places.

These were just the sort of incidents which lent variety to our lives as we carried on with the training.

After Dunkirk, we had an additional job. Frogmen would go out to the Dunkirk beaches at night to bring back rifles, ammunition and any equipment they could retrieve from under the noses of the German Army.

When these brave men had brought back their 'haul', we had to test the ammunition on the range.

We also had to dig trenches and form part of the organisation with the Army in a co-operative effort of defence against a possible invasion.

We put up what fortifications we thought were necessary and they were inspected by an Army General who asked me where our second line of defence was. I replied that we had no second line of defence in the Navy and that, if we were overwhelmed on the first defence line, that was curtains as far as we were concerned. The Navy never retreated.

He wasn't satisfied with this, however, and the Army built a second line of defence further inland, which they manned themselves.

One amazing incident at this time stands out indelibly in my memory for it reveals something of the atmosphere of the time and the strong feelings of the civilians who were in the front line of the fight against the likely invader.

An enemy invader came over and machine gunned the town. It also flew over and strafed a school where the children were out at play in the playground. Quite a number were killed or injured.

Our guns managed to hit the aircraft, shooting away part of a wing, and leaving him to circle slowly around the scene of his attack.

Gradually, he got lower until, finally, he came down to within one hundred yards of the playground he had machine-gunned. But he had not saved himself for the enraged local population set upon him and absolutely tore him limb from limb before the military could stop them.

The Germans, at this time, were laying a new type of mine in the Thames estuary. It was an acoustic mine which brought up underneath a ship and was activated by the ship's own magnetic field.

These new mines were difficult to sweep. You could sweep over the top of them two or three times and nothing would happen – and then a ship would come along and a mine would rise up underneath her and explode.

One night we managed to wing one of the planes that were laying these mines and it came down in mud in the estuary. We put a guard on the aircraft and laid planks of wood across the mud to it.

In due course, along came quite an elderly professor who ignored our planks and waded deep into the mud, scrambled into the aircraft, took what parts he wanted from the mines that were still in the plane, got back into his car and went off to London.

Within twenty-four hours he had the answer to the problem and that was how the famous de-gaussing system of dealing with magnetic mines was born.

The de-gaussing gear consisted of a cable running around the ship reversing the magnetic poles so, instead of attracting the mine up, it repelled it and kept it down on the bottom.

Aeroplanes were also rigged with a metal ring right the way round from the tips of the wings to the tip of the tail. These would fly low over the water and activate the mines which would come up and explode harmlessly behind them.

An oil tanker, which had run the gauntlet at sea right from the Middle East, came in and caught one of these mines. The oiler immediately burst into flames and burnt for three days.

All the crew were killed for the ocean all round the tanker was on fire with the oil and nobody could get near enough to rescue them.

The inferno lit up the whole town by night, making it a marvellous target for the enemy bombers which gave us a hectic time. They could come over and select their target with ease.

One night two American Flying Fortresses just made it back from a trip over Germany and landed on the beach. How they managed to fly back I shall never know for they were absolutely torn to fragments by the shell and shrapnel holes.

These huge planes had to be dismantled where they lay on the beach.

Our Commanding Officer was a Lieutenant Commander and he ran into a different sort of trouble which was nothing to do with the enemy.

I rarely saw much of him. He would be up on the range all day and, at weekends, he would shoot off home. I expect I would have done the same if I hadn't had my wife and child living in Sheerness with me.

The CO used to take home what we called 'rabbits'; tea, sugar, milk, jam and all the things which were either unavailable or rationed for civilians.

On this particular day, a Friday, he decided to set off, as usual, for his weekend, armed with his case full of 'rabbits'. However, he was rather late to catch his train so he decided to get a lift to the station in the dockyard van which delivered our meat.

This van used to have to do two journeys. It first took the meat out to the range where the sailors on course would have their dinner and then it came back with our meat.

Apparently, a detective, or customs officer from the dockyard, decided to travel in the van this day, hiding in the back for the journey out to the range.

On arrival there, the cook cut off a piece of steak and gave it to the van-driver, a civilian, who hid it under his seat. But the customs man was watching and had the driver 'over a barrel'.

However, before he could take him back and charge him, our meat had to be delivered.

I soon got wind that the driver was to be charged with receiving the steak. One of the sailors, in the confusion, stole the steak from under the driver's seat, took it over to the galley and fried it.

That, effectively, removed the evidence against the driver; and very tender it was, too!

But our Commanding Officer, with his case, came along and jumped into the van and asked for a lift to the station.

The detective was only too happy to oblige, especially when he discovered the 'rabbits' in the CO's case. But it was a different kind of station they were heading for, as the CO was returned to HMS *Wildfire* to be detained.

He managed to get word to me and I sent a couple of sailors up to his home to take any evidence that was left.

That Commanding Officer was charged, disciplined, lost seniority and cautioned. He didn't come back to us again and we had a new Lieutenant Commander in charge.

The amazing thing was that after the case, the Customs men brought the evidence back to my office – tins of jam, tea, sugar and everything else – and I sent it out to my wife so that she could use it.

# 31 · Second Time Around

About this time I had word that I was on draft to go as coxswain of one of the tank landing craft for the coming invasion of France. But the Gunnery School people, when they heard of this, decided I was doing more important work where I was, so that idea fell through and Stan stayed put.

We had our fair share of air raids, though, thank God, they didn't do a lot of damage to our barracks. By contrast, the RAF barracks not far away took quite a hammering.

The Germans seemed to know when the British aircraft had come back in to refuel and that was when they would attack.

Eventually, it was discovered that a cook in one of the houses on the RAF station had been passing information to the enemy.

We had quite a number of casualties in our training classes, broken arms or legs and similar injuries. These mostly would occur on the assault course where the men had to clamber along a wire on their stomachs.

Many of them fell off and, invariably, they would fall on their tin helmets or their rifles or some other equally uncomfortable piece of equipment likely to cause injury.

I had one unusual case when a young chap came to me and said he had something sticking out of his stomach. It seemed to have pushed through when he went on the wire.

I examined him and it looked like a piece of a stiff broom sticking out of him. I gave it a pull and he gave a yell, but it didn't come out so I sent him to the HMS *Wildfire* sick bay to see the doctor.

It turned out that the poor fellow had been wounded at Dunkirk and had been taken to an Army emergency hospital for the shrapnel to be taken out of him. They had sewn him up, leaving a ball of cat gut inside him. This had pushed through when he was going across the wire on his stomach.

This incident certainly stirred things up and I think it led to a Court of Inquiry.

Then the 'doodlebugs' started. At first they came over singly but later on, in twos and threes.

We were ordered to fire at them with the anti-aircraft guns, which we did but without much success.

Then they sent up Tempests to try to tip the rockets over with their wings. This turned out to be quite a good method and the fighters downed a good many on to the marshes, thus preventing them from getting through to London.

In fact, a mock town was built on the marshes and this, initially, took a considerable number of bombs. Jerry found it and thought it was an ideal bombing target.

I had sent my wife home during the worst part of the bombing so I was fairly lonely on my own. Mind you, we had plenty of air raids to keep us occupied.

Another reason for sending Laura home was that she was expecting our second child. The baby was a boy – and a bonny boy at that – and when he was about three months old, my wife wanted to come back down to Sheerness.

The bombing had eased – the invasion of France had quietened things down for us with Jerry only finding time for the occasional raid – so back she came.

Things were so easy now that we had time to live a more civilised life and she made many friends. I even grew about half an acre of tomatoes, which were a great success, and I also bred rabbits to supplement the food rations.

In fact, we were really enjoying life. My wife, now surrounded by friends, was almost loth to think of going home after the Armistice was signed. But home she went, and not long after that I was demobbed for the second time.

It seemed I had a lot to look forward to; a civilian life in peacetime, a job to go to, a fine family with two good youngsters and a third now on the way.

A signal had come from *Wildfire* that I was to go for yet another medical and to receive my discharge. Then I was off to Chatham barracks for final payment and the issue of a civilian suit.

I said 'Goodbye' to everybody, the Commanding Officer and all the people with whom I had shared some pretty hair-raising experiences during the hotter days of the war, and away I went to Chatham.

On arrival at the barracks I was 'vitalled up' in the Chief's mess for lunch, had my tot and a good dinner, then went to the clothing store where I had to pick out my suit.

I chose a Navy pin stripe – can you beat that after all those years in uniform – and received a shirt, collar and tie and a hat to complete my civvy rig.

Next port of call was the discharging office and on to the Paymaster's office to receive my pay and gratuity.

The latter came in the form of a Post Office Savings Book from which it was possible only to withdraw £10 at any one time. This was to stop you from blueing it all at once, I suppose.

Anyway, out of the gates I went, a free man and a civilian again.

# 32 · Stan, the Postman

If I really expected life to be a bed of roses back in Civvy Street after the war, I was to be sadly mistaken. At first, anyway, my experiences were to be no better than they had been the first time I left the Navy.

True, after going back to Beccles, I had a month's real holiday during which I redecorated the interior of the house and really got to know my children.

The phrase 'redecorating the house' covers a wide range of jobs, and I never thought I would end up almost re-roofing it.

One night there was a heavy snow storm. It was very fine powdery snow and there was quite a big wind with it.

In the morning, when I woke up, the children called me into their bedrooms to show me that their ceilings were bulging down in a deep curve.

I couldn't think what the devil had happened. I dashed downstairs, got a ladder and went up in the loft. The sight that greeted me was appalling.

Snow, a foot to two foot deep in places, lay thick among the rafters and on the bedroom ceilings.

I got all the available buckets, filled them with snow and lowered them to my wife who dashed downstairs to empty them and return with the buckets for more. It took us a whole morning to clear the snow.

I had to make sure I had got every drop of snow out so that it couldn't melt and soak through into the bedrooms. The ceilings, marvellously, went back into shape, I've no idea how.

But I had to devise a way of plugging the gaps under the tiles for there was no roofing felt at all. The tiles, which were on small studs, were just laid on the roof.

We got all the rags we could find in the house and tore them into strips. Then my wife went around to the neighbours to collect what rags they could spare. These we also tore into strips.

Then I put on an overcoat, a pair of diver's stockings and sea boots and went back up into the loft, armed with a chisel.

Using the chisel to push the strips of rag into place, I plugged every gap on the roof. It took me two long cold days of working by the light of candles set on the rafters, but I finished the job and was jolly glad when I had.

It not only stopped the snow from coming through but it also made the bedrooms a few degrees warmer. It was a primitive kind of insulation, you might say.

After my leave I went back to the Post Office and, from the pay point of view, came down to earth with a bump. All I was getting at the Post Office was £7.10s a week on which we had to bring up our family. For Laura and I it was quite a struggle.

We supplemented our income, as long as we could, with the gratuity money from that Post Office bank book, but as time went on things really got tough.

What didn't help matters was the fact that I hated the Post Office. Somehow, after a life at sea, it didn't seem to fit me. I couldn't bear the smell of letters, or the duties, which were quite long and arduous.

At that time we had three collections and deliveries a day, which meant you could be on the go from five in the morning to seven at night. There was also an early morning duty which started at 3 am.

There would be two people on this duty and each had a key. There was a double lock on the door so one couldn't go in without the other. If one was late, the other had to wait or go round and call him up.

The duty consisted of sorting up the overnight mail and getting Halesworth and Southwold letters and parcels ready for the van.

For me, the most arduous duty was the all night one. It consisted of taking the large van from Beccles, first to Harleston – where you had to unlock the Post Office and load up the mail, then lock the office again – and then on to Diss to catch the London-bound mail train.

Once the mail had been loaded on to the train and it had departed for London you had a long wait ahead of you – which included a meal and a couple of cups of tea – until the train from London came in at 2.30 am.

The job then was to unload the mail from the train and put it in the van, Southwold mail first, then Halesworth, then Beccles and finally Harleston.

Then back you went, stopping at Harleston to unlock the Post Office, throw in the mail and lock it up again, and back to Beccles.

But the shift still wasn't over. Having unloaded the Beccles mail, the van had to pick up the letters and parcels that had been sorted there and add them to the mail it already carried for Halesworth and Southwold, then deliver it to the Post Offices in those towns.

It would be around 9 am when the van and driver would arrive wearily back at Beccles, only to find, invariably, that someone had gone sick or was on holiday and the Post Office was short staffed. So you would be needed to do a delivery in the town and that would extend your shift until about 10.30 am when you finally went home for breakfast.

Come to think of it, though, the town duties were pretty bad as well. You started at 5 am, sorted up all the mail, then you would lay in your own round and go out to deliver at 9 am.

Deliveries were quite long and tiring and the postmen had no trolley in those days to carry the large amount of mail which went in the sack on his back. Stamps, you see, were only a penny ha'penny or tuppence in those days – less than 4p or 5p in today's money.

After your delivery you got a break of an hour for breakfast, then it was back to the Post Office for the next delivery. In the afternoon there was a tea break before you went out on the third delivery. By the end of your working day you had probably walked twenty miles or more.

I was made secretary of the local branch of the Post Office Union and one of the first jobs I took on was to re-arrange the leave roster.

All the summer months used to be taken up by the senior postmen. They had first choice for their holiday dates and, consequently, took the best months, leaving everybody else with never a chance of getting a summer holiday at all.

I arranged a rota system whereby the bottom four names would go up to the top next year so that everybody had a fair chance of getting the best leave dates.

This idea was quite popular and was approved by the Postmaster, so we were all ship-shape on that score. But I had one chap who continually came to me with complaints. He was the sort of person for whom nothing was ever right.

The trouble was that as soon as I would take up his complaint with the Postmaster, this awkward fellow would back down and fail to confirm he had made the complaint in the first place.

Well, I can't avoid admitting that one day I lost my temper with him, I grabbed hold of him and stuck him head first in one of the mail bags which hung, invitingly, wide open from four hooks on a frame. It was no great feat of strength, especially to an ex-matelot who was all riled up.

I was in the act of tying up the mailbag and sealing it – for I would willingly, at that moment, have sent him off to London, with or without the postmark – but I was restrained by the rest of the staff.

After this, I should add, chummy and me became the best of friends and everything went much more smoothly and with fewer complaints.

I made the best of a bad job in the Post Office. We had a good few laughs despite the fact that I hated the job.

When I was sixty I had to retire and that was when I made a real faux pas.

My time expired on 23 March so I thought I would have a week's leave, which was due to me, after that date so that I got an extra week's money with which to start my retirement. But it was not to be.

Somebody suddenly unearthed a rule – which no one seemed to have heard of before – that you had to take your leave before retiring from the Post Office, so I lost a week's pay and a week's leave.

After I retired the local newspaper editor, Mr Gerald Lawson, came and interviewed me and gave me quite a good write-up. The Post Office presented me with a set of cutlery which we still have.

I had been paid off, you might say, to go into the Reserves.

# 33 · Into Reserve

I prefer to think of my departure from the Post Office as going into reserve rather than retirement because I couldn't bear to think of having nothing to do and having no prospects of finding some useful way of occupying my time.

I certainly found work, but I also found that the Battle of Jutland, all those years ago, was getting ready to catch up with me again. The ghosts of these long dead battleships of the British and German High Seas Fleets were to haunt me again in the leg wound I sustained during that far off and indecisive battle.

For the moment, however, in those early days after leaving the Post Office, time hung heavily on my hands. I did all the jobs I had promised to do in the house and garden and, after that, I was just fed up with nothing much to do. So I started looking for another little job.

Luckily for me, one eventually turned up with a storage company operating at Ellough, on a former wartime airfield just outside Beccles.

My job consisted of keeping account of the stores which we had on the premises and the amount of grain, the number of bags and the weight, so that the correct charges could be made to the companies which were our customers.

Wages and accounts were worked out by a firm of accountants in Lowestoft but, after about a year, the boss suggested that I do the accounts and wages as this would save him quite a bit of money.

This I agreed to do, for a couple of pounds extra a week, and I took over the company's accounts, lock, stock and barrel.

Meanwhile, the company began to grow quite rapidly and the old airfield was quickly becoming quite a substantial industrial estate with other firms like Fibrenyle, Fison's, Beechams and the Co-op becoming involved or joining our growing list of customers.

We installed two driers to dry the grain. We also used a large hangar which we had re-sheathed, to dry and store grain.

But we had so much need for more and more buildings, because the storage and drying of grain was such a bulky business, that we decided eventually to give up the grain business and concentrate entirely on hiring out storage space to companies for other commodities.

I had never done wages or accounts before, but, like everything else, you can get used to it quite quickly.

My daughter, who is an accomplished shorthand-typist, gave me lessons on the typewriter and I got quite efficient, using two or three fingers instead of one.

Business continued to improve until we became quite a substantial organisation out at Ellough and my time was very fully occupied.

But, after about six years, I began to get trouble with my old leg wound. At first, I thought it was probably cramp, but I was persuaded to go to the doctor and he sent me to a specialist who diagnosed artery trouble.

I had to go into hospital in Norwich where the old leg came under the surgeons' scrutiny again. They simply took the main vein out, cleaned it and put it back. It was a marvellous job and it enabled me to walk normally again, only having to stop every hundred yards or so to let the blood circulate.

While I was convalescing the firm kept paying me and, for somebody at my time of life, it was good to feel needed. In fact, they finally brought the accounts and wages, and a typewriter, round to my home so I could help keep things going while I was still convalescent.

They would telephone through the information, or the foreman would bring me all the latest news and accounts, and I would sit at home and work through them.

I was convalescent, I suppose, for about two months and they begged me to go back to the job, promising to provide transport to and from work.

So I went back and I continued working out there until I was seventy four when I finally decided it was time to retire. I had already retired once, of course – from the Post Office – but it seems I have made a lifetime habit of doing things twice; especially retiring.

In any case, decimalisation had come in and it was too much of a worry for me to cope with the new money.

At this time my wife and I were living in Station Road, Beccles, in a large house which seemed to be full of stairs. There were steps up to the front door, down into the kitchen and down again into the basement. And, of course, there was the staircase to the bedrooms.

My bed had to be brought down to the ground floor and my wife and I slept in one of the front rooms because the stairs were too much for me.

The children had all married and left home, so there we were rattling about in a large house with a wonderful garden which I could not control, just Darby and Joan, Laura and Stan.

So we looked around for something smaller and, as luck would have it, a vacancy occurred in the Woodhill Memorial Bungalows in Grove Road, Beccles. We put in for it, my wife went to see the chairman of the society that runs the group of homes and we got it.

I thank God for that because it enabled us to live, just the two of us, in a small bungalow, just comfortable together and with no hard housework.

This is my story. I am now in my eighties and I have had a wonderful life. I have been lucky to combine a good family life with an adventurous naval and civilian career.

My wife and I are ideally happy. We have three lovely children, all married, comfortable and all successful in life, and four lovely grandchildren, two boys and two girls. What more could we wish and we thank God for it all.

As for old Stan himself – well, it's true there has been more trouble with my leg. I have been in hospital again and had a pretty rough time.

Those ghostly battleships of Jutland, the jailers in the Black Hole of Baku, the steamy heat of the Amazon Jungle; all these spirits of a life of adventure will keep fighting over my weatherbeaten body until I finally get paid off for the last time.

When I go out these days – perhaps to a meeting of the Royal Ancient Order of Buffaloes to which I belong – I have to get a lift or go in a wheel-chair with Laura doing the navigating.

But I have got the meetings of my local branch of the Royal Naval Association, which I am glad to say was formed recently at Beccles, and I can share memories with my 'oppos'.

And I still am a regular reader of the *Navy News*, the monthly paper that keeps me in touch with today's Royal Navy. It shows me still that the men who sail Her Majesty's ships prove themselves, in actions like the Falklands war, worthy successors to my generation and those who went before. Good for them.

Now I am securely tied up alongside with my memories. If you can't exactly be a man of action any more, the next best thing is to remember the times when you were and to live through them all again. That way you get the best out of a good life.

I ran away from home and went to sea all those years ago. And I saw the world, the best and the worst of it. And if I had my time to live through again, I wouldn't change anything.